An easy-to-use survey of the
New Testament that shows you
how to put each biblical book
in perspective—

- helps you learn with
  illustrations, outlines, daily
  readings and many other
  study aids

- explains how the Bible
  was written and why

- gets you into the Bible
  and gets the Bible into
  you!

HENRIETTA C. MEARS

WHAT THE
NEW
TESTAMENT
IS ALL ABOUT

Regal
Books

A Division of GL Publications
Ventura, CA U.S.A.

The translation of all Regal books is under the direction of GLINT. GLINT provides technical help for the adaptation, translation and publishing of books for millions of people worldwide. For information regarding translation contact: GLINT, P.O. Box 6688, Ventura, California 93006.

Fourteenth Printing, 1983

Published by Regal Books
A Division of GL Publications
Ventura, California 93006
Printed in U.S.A.

ISBN 0-8307-0525-2

CHRIST, THE LIVING WORD

The New Testament is an account of a *Man*. God Himself became a man so that we might know what to think of when we think of God (John 1:14; 14:9). His appearance on the earth is the central event of all history. The Old Testament sets the stage for it. The New Testament describes it.

As a man Christ *lived* the most perfect life ever known. He was kind, tender, gentle, patient, and sympathetic. He loved people. He worked marvelous miracles to feed the hungry. Multitudes, weary, pain-ridden and heartsick, came to Him, and He gave them rest (Matthew 11:28-30). It is said that if all the deeds of kindness that He did were written, the world would not contain the books (John 21:25).

Then: He *died*—to take away the sin of the world, and to become the Saviour of men.

Then: He *rose* from the dead. He is *alive* today. He is not merely an historical character, but a living Person—the most important fact of history, and the most vital force in the world today. And He promised eternal life to all who come to Him.

The writers of the New Testament reveal to us the character and teachings of Jesus Christ, the mediator of the New Covenant. There were at least eight of these men, four of whom—Matthew, John, Peter and Paul—were apostles; two—Mark and Luke—were companions of the apostles; and two—James and Jude—were brothers of Jesus. The books were written at various times during the second half of the first century. Much light is thrown on the writings of these men in *What the New Testament Is All About*.

I

INTRODUCTION

Have you ever climbed a very high mountain and upon arriving at the summit were thrilled with the breath-taking view? While traveling through the valleys you had seen the details — the tree, the flower, the brook and the stone. But from the mountaintop you had a panoramic view of the vast expanses of God's wonderful nature. This survey of the Bible is planned to give you such a panoramic view of the inspired Word of God, the Holy Bible. From this viewpoint you will see it as a cohesive whole instead of as a series of unrelated stories or details.

The Bible is the story of what God is doing in history. Like any good story, it has a beginning and an ending. It starts with the creation; conflict is introduced with the workings of Satan and the fall of man, introducing the dilemma. The rest of the story is the solving of that grand dilemma by God, and the final triumph of His purpose at the second coming of Christ. All the events in between fit into that story and contribute to the unfolding of the "plot." The Bible has one main theme — redemption — and many sub-themes which run through the entire book. Redemption is hinted at in the beginning — Genesis 3:15 — and developed as the main subject, coming to a climax with the advent of Christ. The sub-themes, interwoven into the narrative, and all dependent upon the main theme, redemption, are defined and illustrated in the events of the Bible.

Along with this panoramic view of the Bible goes the *specific* lesson to be found in each book. Of course, there are nearly as many lessons to be drawn as there are verses; but rather than doing that kind of detailed study, this volume aims to give an inclusive picture of the New Testament and the general lessons to be drawn from each book.

Fortunately, the twentieth-century thirst for knowledge includes in America a wholesome curiosity about what the Bible teaches. In accompaniment to churches' expanding Sunday School enrollments, home Bible-study groups are springing up and churches gladly respond to desires for weekday classes.

Such groups find this volume and its companion, *What the Old Testament Is All About,* to be admirably suited for study guides. They are in fact abridgments of a parent volume, *What the Bible Is All About,* which has proved an excellent teaching tool for instructors.

In reading the book now in your hand remember that it is a wonderful privilege to have and to hold the precious Word of God. People of other days have been denied this privilege. Even now, in some nations, the Bible is a forbidden book and the public teaching of it is considered a crime against the state. In pagan lands millions have never had the opportunity of hearing its message or reading its pages. It is therefore not only your privilege but also your sacred responsibility to study the Scriptures. You will find *What the New Testament Is All About* a great aid in this essential study. Accept this privilege and responsibility seriously. Carefully follow the directions found in this book. Become acquainted with the characters portrayed in God's holy revelation.

The daily Bible readings will lead you step by step into an understanding of the sixty-six books of Holy Scripture. Check the progress you are making by using the review questions found at the end of each section of your book. As you conscientiously use this *What the New Testament Is All About,* you will find yourself becoming *approved unto God, a workman that needeth not to be ashamed, rightly dividing the word of truth* (II Timothy 2:15).

CONTENTS

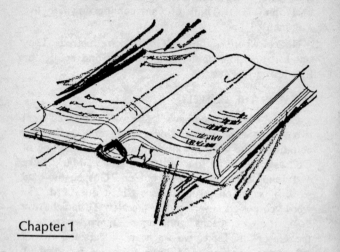

Chapter 1

LET'S LOOK AT THE GOSPELS

THE GOSPELS PORTRAY JESUS CHRIST,
OUR SAVIOUR AND LORD

He is here! The promised One has come! Who has come? The One whom all the prophets have foretold, Jesus Christ, the Lord.

Every prophet in the Old Testament assured God's chosen people again and again that a Messiah should come who would be the King of the Jews. They therefore looked forward with passionate longing and patriotism to the coming of that King with pomp and power.

We read in Isaiah 7:14: *Therefore the Lord Himself shall give you a sign; Behold, a virgin shall conceive, and bear a son, and shall call His name Immanuel,* God

1

with us. This is just the One that the evangelists tell us about. The Gospels present Jesus in our midst. John says, *The Word was made flesh, and dwelt among us* (John 1:14). Think of God coming down to live with men!

Notice where the four Gospels are placed. They stand at the close of the Old Testment and before the Epistles.

WHAT IS THE GOSPEL?

Gospel means "good news." The word is derived from two Anglo-Saxon words, God (good) and spell, story or tidings. The good news concerning Jesus, the Son of God, is given us by four writers, Matthew, Mark, Luke and John, although there is but one Gospel, the glad story of salvation through Jesus Christ our Lord. The word "gospel" is never used in the New Testament of a book. It always means "good news." When we speak of the Gospel of Luke, we ought to understand that it means the good news of Jesus Christ as recorded by Luke. Nevertheless, from the earliest times, the term "gospel" has been applied to each of the four narratives which record the life of Christ.

No doubt originally the good news was oral. Men went from one place to another, telling the glad story by word of mouth. After a while a written record was necessary. More than one attempted this, with no success. See what Luke says in Luke 1:1-4: *For as much as many have taken in hand to set forth in order a declaration of those things which are most surely believed among us, Even as they delivered them unto us, which from the beginning were eyewitnesses, and ministers of the Word; It seemed good to me also, having had perfect understanding of all things from the very first, to write unto thee in order, most excellent Theophilus, That thou mightest know the certainty of those things, wherein thou hast been instructed.*

WHY FOUR GOSPELS?

As everyone knows, there are four Gospels, but the question at once arises, "Why four?" Why wouldn't one straightforward, continuous narrative have been enough? Would not this have been simpler and clearer? Might this not have saved us from some of the difficulties which have arisen in what some have said are conflicting accounts?

The answer seems plain. Because one or two would not have given us a complete portrayal of the life of Christ. He is presented as:

> King in Matthew
> Servant in Mark
> Son of Man in Luke
> Son of God in John

It is true that each of the four Gospels has much in common with the others. Each deals with Christ's earthly ministry, His death and resurrection. His teachings and miracles, but each Gospel has its differences. We at once see that each of the writers is trying to present a different picture of our one Lord.

Matthew deliberately adds to his account what Mark omits. There is a lack of completeness as to His life history in any one of the four Gospels, or in all taken together. Hear what John says in 21:25: *And there are also many other things which Jesus did, the which, if they should be written every one, I suppose that even the world itself could not contain the books that should be written.*

In the National Gallery in London there are three representations on a single canvas of Charles I. In one his head is turned to the right; in another, to the left; and in the center we find the full face view. This is the story of this production. Van Dyck painted them for Bernini, the Roman sculptor, that he might by their help make a bust of the king. By combining the impressions so received, Bernini would be better able to produce a "speaking" likeness. One view would not have been enough.

It may be true that the Gospels were intended to serve the very purpose of these portraits. Each presents a different aspect of our Lord's life on earth. Together we have the complete picture. He was a King, but He was the Perfect Servant, too. He was the Son of Man, but we must not forget He was the Son of God.

The four Gospels present the person and work of our blessed Saviour, but each in a distinct relationship. Let us give one more illustration that we feel will help to clarify what we mean. Suppose that four men would undertake to write a "life" of Theodore Roosevelt, and that each chose to represent him as a different character. One would treat of his private and domestic life; a second would deal with him as a sportsman and hunter of big game; a third would tell of his military prowess; and the fourth would trace his political and presidential career. You can see at once that each of his biographers would be looking for and recording only those things which would help develop his story. Each would use only that material which helped paint the side of the man he was describing.

**Master this outline and you will be familiar
with the contents of the Gospels for life.**

JESUS IN THE FOUR GOSPELS

King Matthew presents Jesus as King. Written primarily for the Jews, He is the Son of David. His royal genealogy is given in chapter 1. In chapters 5-7, in the Sermon on the Mount, we have the manifesto of the King, containing the laws of His kingdom.

Servant Mark depicts Jesus as Servant. Written to the Romans, there is no genealogy. Why? Men are not interested in the genealogy of a servant. More miracles are found here than in any other Gospel. Romans cared little for words; far more for deeds.

BIBLE LANDS

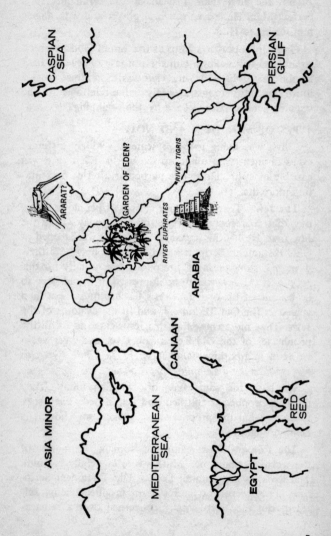

Man Luke sets forth Jesus as the perfect Man. Written to the Greeks, His genealogy goes back to Adam, the first man, instead of to Abraham. As a perfect Man, He is seen much in prayer and with angels ministering to Him.

God John portrays Jesus as the Son of God. Written to all who will believe with the purpose of leading men to Christ (John 20:31), everything in this Gospel illustrates and demonstrates His divine relationship. The opening verse carries us back to "the beginning."

TYPES OF MEN THEN AND NOW

Christ was going to be presented to widely different types of men, who made up the world. Each race was capable of appreciating one particular kind of presentation more than another.

The Jew—There were four classes of people in Jesus' day that represent four types of men today. Take the Jew first. He had his special training. He was steeped in Old Testament Scripture and the prophets. Matthew wrote the story of Jesus' life on earth especially for this people. If the Jew was to be impressed, it would have to be by one of his own race. His teacher must be a man versed in the Old Testament, and in the customs of the Jews. They must know that this Jesus came to fulfill the prophecies of the Old Testament. Over and over again we read in Matthew, *That it might be fulfilled . . . as was spoken by Jeremiah the prophet . . .*

We have the same type of Christian today. They revel in prophecies fulfilled and unfulfilled. They seek to know what the prophets have spoken, and how it is being brought to pass.

The Roman—Next came the Roman, the master of the world at that time. Mark wrote especially for him. The Romans knew nothing about Old Testament Scripture. They were not interested in prophecy being fulfilled. But they were vitally concerned over a remarkable Leader who had appeared in Palestine. He had claimed more than ordinary authority, and had possessed extraordinary powers. They wanted to hear more about this Jesus. What sort of a person He really was; what He said, and what He had done.

The Roman liked the straightforward message of one like Mark. One thousand three hundred and seventy-five times the word "and" is used in Mark. It moves on in beauty and force all its own. Mark's Gospel is filled with deeds, not words. Clearly it is the Gospel of the Ministry of Christ.

The Roman of Jesus' day was a type of the average businessman of today. He is not concerned at first about the genealogy of a king, but with a God "who is able"; a God who can meet man's every need. Mark is the businessman's Gospel.

The Greek—Then there is Luke. This Gospel was written by a Greek doctor, to his own countrymen who were lovers of beauty, poetry and culture. They lived in a world of large ideas. Their tastes were fastidious. The Gospel of Luke tells of the birth and childhood of Jesus. It gives the inspired songs connected with the life of Christ. We find the salutation of Elizabeth when Mary visited her. (Luke 1:42-45) We hear the song of the virgin mother. (Luke 1:46-55) Even Zacharias burst into praise when speech was restored to him. (Luke 1:68-79) At the Saviour's birth a chorus of angel voices ring out (Luke 2:13,14), and then the shepherd's song of praise to God in Luke 2:20 is heard.

The Greek is the type of the student and idealist today who is seeking after truth, for he believes that is the goal of happiness.

All Men—John is written to all men, that they might believe that Jesus is the Christ. Christ is portrayed as the Son of God. This Gospel is filled with extraordinary claims that attest His divine character and mission.

The "all men" of John's day were like the masses today who need Christ. They include the "whosoevers" who will believe on the Lord Jesus Christ because they have a sense of need and want to receive the gift of eternal life through Jesus Christ the Lord.

When we draw nearer, we then see good reason for four Gospels. Why four, when Christ is the one glorious Theme of them all? Each of the writers is absorbed with some special feature in Christ's character and office. Each evangelist takes some office and develops it with convincing power. It is the unfolding of this particular view of the work of Christ that stamps the design on each book and distinguishes it from the others.

Minimum Daily Requirements / Spiritual Vitamins

Sunday: THE KING CHRIST JESUS Matthew 2:1-12; 21:1-11

Monday: THE SERVANT CHRIST JESUS Mark 10:35-45; 2:1-22

Tuesday: THE MAN CHRIST JESUS Luke 4:1-13; John 19:4-13

Wednesday: THE GOD-MAN John 1:1-18; 3:1-16

Thursday: OUR REDEEMER, JESUS CHRIST John 19:16-42

Friday: THE MASTER, JESUS CHRIST Matthew 4:18-25

Saturday: OUR MASTER, JESUS CHRIST John 21:1-17

Chapter 2

LET'S LOOK AT MATTHEW

MATTHEW PORTRAYS JESUS CHRIST,
THE PROMISED MESSIAH

COMING OF THE KING (Read Matthew 1:1–2:23)

The main purpose of the Spirit in this book is to show that Jesus of Nazareth is the Messiah predicted by Moses and the prophets.

All the maps of the world and all the calendars of time tell of Christ's birthplace and birthday. We don't have to build the story out of the imagination. We are given names and dates. Christianity is a historical religion. The Gospel does not begin with, "Once upon a time," but starts with "Bethlehem in Judea." The town is there, and we can know the very place where Jesus was born. The time is definite, "in the days of Herod the king."

9

Most people, whenever they begin reading Matthew, with its "begats," and Luke 3:23-38, with its "the son of's," wonder what these are all about. We ought to realize that if they were included in Scripture they were put there for a purpose.

A "genealogy" is "the history of the descent of an individual or family from an ancestor" (Webster). There are two genealogies of Christ: Matthew 1:1-17, and Luke 3:23-38. They are not alike, and the reason is that each one traces the descent of Christ back for different purposes.

Matthew traces Christ's line back to Abraham and David to show that He was a JEW (coming from David).

Luke traces Christ's line back to Adam to show that He belonged to the human race.

Matthew alone tells of the visit of the wise men from the East. These were Persian magi, scholars, students of the stars. They came to worship and honor a King. These wise men did not come inquiring, "Where is He that is born the Saviour of the World?" but *Where is He that is born King of the Jews?*

The birth of Jesus was followed by twelve years of silence until His visit with the doctors in Jerusalem. Then silence shut Him in again, with only the word "carpenter" to throw any light upon the next eighteen years, and let us know what He was doing. Jesus took thirty years of preparation for three years of ministry.

This is a great lesson for all of us today. Many of us chafe under years of training. We do not realize the value that God places on preparedness. All through the Bible leaders went through a period of getting ready before their great work was done. Think of Abraham, Joseph, Moses, Joshua, Esther and others. Time is never wasted in preparation. If we are prepared for a task, we can do it quickly and well.

PROCLAMATION OF THE KINGDOM
(Read Matthew 3:1–16:20)

In Matthew we hear the "Voice": *Repent ye: for the kingdom of heaven is at hand ... Prepare ye the way of the Lord, make His paths straight* (Matthew 3:2,3).

The King must be announced! It was the duty of this herald to go before the King, as a Roman officer before his ruler, and command that the roads be repaired over which his master would travel. John the Baptist did this. He showed that the spiritual roads of the lives of men and nations were full of the chuck-holes of sin and sharp turns of iniquity, and needed rebuilding and straightening.

We see the King stepping from His personal and private life into His public ministry. (Matthew 4) He is facing a crisis. Satan met Him. Notice that Satan offered Jesus a short cut to that universal Kingdom which He had come to gain through the long and painful way of the cross, but Christ came to be a Saviour first, then a King. How strong is the temptation to take a short cut to our ambitions! Jesus stood victor. His shield undented and untarnished. He went forth to conquer all other temptations until His final victory and ascension to heaven as Lord of all. (See I Cor. 10:13.)

Every kingdom must have its laws and standards to control its subjects. The Kingdom of Heaven is no exception. Jesus declared that He came not to destroy the law but to fulfill it. From the lofty pulpit of a mountain, Jesus preached the sermon that contains the laws of His Kingdom. (Matthew 5–7) Read through these chapters and refresh your memory about this most wonderful of Jesus' discourses. Many a person who is not a Christian claims that the Sermon on the Mount is his creed. How little he understands the depth of its meaning. It is important that we do not simply praise this rule as a wonderful theory but that we actually practice it in our own lives. The root of this law is kindness. It is true, if human society would have its standards as theirs, the world would be set in order. One day filled with it would be a bit of heaven. Love would reign instead of lawlessness. Christ shows us that sin lies not just in committing the act but in the motive behind it as well. (See Matthew 5:21,22,27,28.) The Sermon on the Mount sets forth the Constitution of the Kingdom.

We find the King proved by the special miracles which He wrought. (Matthew 8; 9) He met human needs. There are twelve astonishing miracles in these two chapters. What were they?

Jesus not only preached Himself, but He gathered others around Him. It was necessary to organize His Kingdom, to put it on a wider and more permanent basis. A king must have subjects. Jesus still has a great message for the world, and He needs us to carry it. Spiritual ideas cannot stalk alone through the world and be of any value. They must be clothed with men and institutions who will serve as hearts and brains, hands and feet to carry them out. This is what Jesus was doing. He was calling men into His companionship to train them to carry on His work.

Where did Jesus find His helpers? Not in the temple, among the doctors or priests, nor in the colleges of Jerusalem. He found them on the seashore mending their nets. Jesus did not call many mighty or noble, but rather chose the foolish things of the world to confound the wise. (I Cor. 1:27) A list of the disciples is given in Matthew 10:2-4.

Note some of the warnings and instructions for the disciples which Jesus stated in Matthew 10. What were they? If these requirements of discipleship hold true today, can you call yourself a disciple?

PALESTINE
NEW TESTAMENT

SIDON
ITURAEA
ABILENE
SAREPTA
DAMASCUS
TYRE
MT. HERMON
CAESAREA PHILIPPI
PHOENICIA
TRACHONITIS

MEDITERRANEAN
SEA
GALILEE
GAULANITIS
CHORAZIN
PTOLEMAIS
CAPERNAUM
BETHSAIDA
CANA
SEA OF
GALILEE
RIVER
KISHON
MAGDALA
TIBERIAS
GERGESA?
NAZARETH
MT. OF
BEATITUDES
RIVER
KISHON
GADARA
NAIN
RIVER
JORDAN
DECAPOLIS
CAESAREA
SALIM?
AENON?
SAMARIA
SAMARIA
PLAIN OF
SHARON
SYCHAR
MT. GERIZIM
ANTIPATRIS
BETHABARA?
JOPPA
ARIMATHEA
EPHRAIM
PERAEA
RAMAH
LYDDA
EMMAUS
JERICHO
BETHPHAGE?
BETHANY?
AZOTUS
JERUSALEM
MT. OF OLIVES
BETHANY
BETHLEHEM
JUDAEA
DEAD SEA
GAZA
IDUMAEA
EGYPT
ARABIA

The word kingdom occurs some 55 times in Matthew. The expression "kingdom of heaven," is found 35 times here and nowhere else in the Gospels. Of the fifteen parables recorded in Matthew, all but three begin, *The kingdom of heaven is like* . . . Jesus likened the Kingdom of Heaven to: The Sower, The Tares, A Mustard Seed, Leaven in the Dough, A Hid Treasure, A Pearl of Great Price, A Dragnet. (Matthew 13)

These parables, called *the mysteries of the kingdom of heaven* (Matthew 13:11), describe what the result of the presence of the Gospel of Christ in the world will be during this present age until the time of His return when He will gather the harvest. (Matthew 13:40-43) We see no bright picture of a converted world. There shall be tares mixed with the wheat, good fish and bad, leaven in the loaf. Then there is an abnormal growth of the mustard seed, that admits "fowls of the air" to lodge in its branches. This is Christendom. Only Christ can determine what is good and what is bad, and at the harvest He will divide. If we are to have a kingdom on this earth, with the laws which Christ set down, then we must have the King. Some day Christ will come in power and great glory and establish His throne on this earth. We will have peace when the Prince of Peace reigns!

REJECTION OF KING (Read Matthew 16:21—20:34)

The sad story reads that Christ *came unto His own, and His own received Him not* (John 1:11). The Kingdom was first presented to the rightful heirs, the children of Israel (Jews), but they refused the offer, rejected the King, and finally crucified Him. From Matthew 12 on, we see much controversy among the leaders concerning Jesus.

Why did the Jews refuse the Kingdom? The world today is longing intensely for the golden age. A millennium of peace and rest is the great desire of diplomats and rulers. But they want it in their own way and on their own terms. They desire to bring it about by their own efforts. They have no longing for a millennium brought about by the personal return on earth of the Lord Jesus Christ. It was just so with the Jews in the days of John the Baptist.

Have you put Christ on the throne of your life? Have you the peace you long for? Have you accepted Christ's terms for your life?

Only in Matthew's Gospel is the "Church" named. When the Kingdom was rejected we find a change in the teachings of Jesus. He began to talk about the "Church" instead of the Kingdom. (Matthew 16:18) Church comes from the word "ecclesia" which means "called out ones." Because His own would not accept Him as King, Christ said He was calling out anyone who would believe, Jew or Gentile, to belong to His Church, which is His body. He began to lay plans for the building of a new edifice, a new body of people, which would include both Jew and Gentile. (Eph. 2:14-18)

When they were far away from the busy scene in which they lived, Jesus asked His disciples the question: *Whom do men say that I the Son of man am?*

This is the important question today! First asked by an obscure Galilean in that far off solitude, it has come thundering down through the centuries and has become the world's mightiest question. What think ye of Christ? What men think determines what they do and are. The ideas men hold about industry, wealth, government, morals and religion mold society and alter lives. So what men think of Christ is the master force in the world today and more than anything else influences life and thought and civilizations.

The disciples gave the answers to this important

question that the men of their day were giving. The answers then were as varied as they now are. All agreed that Jesus was an extraordinary person, at least a prophet or a teacher with an element of the supernatural. Men's opinions of Christ are high. The answer that Jesus was a myth, a dupe, or an impostor, is no longer tolerated.

Jesus now turned the general question into the sharp personal inquiry. *But whom say ye that I am?* Ask yourself this question. Important as the general question is, far more important to each one of us is this personal question. No one can escape it. A neutral answer is impossible. He is either God or an impostor.

Thou art the Christ, the Son of the living God! exclaimed the impulsive, fervent Peter. This confession is great because it exalts Christ as the Son of God and crowns Him with deity. He said to Peter and the disciples, after this answer concerning who He was, *Upon this rock I will build my church.* This is what Christ was going to do—build a Church of which He Himself was to be the chief cornerstone. This Church was born on Pentecost. (Acts 2)

For the first time the fateful shadow of the cross fell across the path of the disciples. From this time on Jesus began to draw back the curtain that veiled the future and to show His disciples the things that would come to pass. (See Matthew 16:21.)

TRIUMPH OF THE KING
(Read Matthew 21:1–28:20)

On the morning of Palm Sunday crowds were gathering along the road leading to Jerusalem. Jesus was to enter the city that day. This little parade could not have been compared in magnificence with many a procession that has attended the coronation of a king, or the inauguration of a president; but it meant much more for the world. Jesus for the first time permitted a public recognition and celebration of His rights as Messiah-King. The end was approaching with awful swiftness, and He must offer Himself as Messiah, even if only to be rejected.

In the evening the crowds dispersed, and Jesus quietly returned to Bethany. Apparently nothing in the way of making Jesus King had been accomplished. His "hour had not yet come." Christ must be Saviour first, then come again as King of kings and Lord of lords.

Christ's authority is brought into question as He goes into the temple and orders the merchants out, overturning their tables and telling them that they have made the house of God a den of thieves. A bitter controversy follows. *Then went the Pharisees, and took counsel how they might entangle Him in His talk* (Matthew 22:15). He bids farewell to Jerusalem until He will come again to sit on David's throne.

He delivers His Mount Olivet discourse. He foretells the condition of the world after His ascension until He comes back in glory, to judge the nations as to their treatment of His brethren, the Jews. (Matthew 25)

Much of Jesus' discourse in Matthew 24 and 25 is devoted to His second coming. He exhorts men to be ready, in the parables of the faithful servants, then ten virgins, and of the talents.

We have been passing through some of the highlights in the life of King Jesus; now we step into the shadows as we enter Gethsemane. Although a large number of disciples believed in Jesus and followed Him, the opposition of the Jews was bitter and they determined to put Him to death. On the grounds of blasphemy, and of claiming to be the King of the Jews, thus making Himself the enemy of the Roman Emperor, Jesus was delivered up by Pilate to be crucified.

Matthew is not alone in his record of the terrible

circumstances of the Saviour's passion; but he makes us feel that in the mock array, the crown of thorns, the sceptre, the title over the cross, we have a witness, though it be only scorn, to the kingly claim.

After hanging on the cruel tree for six hours, the Saviour died, not from physical suffering alone, but of a broken heart, for He bore the sins of the whole world. We hear His triumphant cry, *It is finished!* He paid the debt of sin and became the world's Redeemer!

But this is not all of the redemption story. Jesus was put in Joseph's tomb, and on the third day He arose, as He had said. This is the supreme triumph of His kingship. Men thought that He was dead and His Kingdom had failed. By His resurrection, God assured His disciples that the King still lived and that one day He would come back to establish His Kingdom on earth.

The ascension of Jesus is not recorded in Matthew. The curtain falls with the Messiah still on earth, for it is on earth and not in heaven, that the Son of David is yet to reign in glory. The last time the Jews saw Christ, He was on the Mount of Olives. The next time they will see Him, He will be on the Mount of Olives! See Zechariah 14:4; also Acts 1:11.

Jesus has announced His program and a crisis has struck in the history of Christianity. The climax is found in the great commission, *All power is given unto me in heaven and in earth. Go ye therefore, and teach all nations, baptizing them in the name of the Father, and of the Son, and of the Holy Ghost: Teaching them to observe all things whatsoever I have commanded you: and, lo, I am with you alway, even unto the end of the world.* (Matthew 28:18-20)

On what mission were they sent? To overrun the world with armies and make men submit under the sword? No, but to *make disciples of all nations.*

From the mountain top of His ascension His disciples started forth on this mission, radiating from that center, and they have gone on until they have everywhere reached the rim of the world. Christianity is no national or racial religion. It knows no bounds of mountain or sea but it envelopes the globe.

CHRIST'S COMING

With Angels

When the Son of man shall come in His glory, and all the holy angels with Him. (Matthew 25:31)

With Rewards

The Son of man shall come in the glory of His Father with His angels; and then He shall reward every man according to his works. (Matthew 16:27)

In Glory

Whosoever therefore shall be ashamed of me . . . of him also shall the Son of man be ashamed, when He cometh in the glory of His Father with the holy angels. (Mark 8:38)

In Power

They shall see the Son of man coming in the clouds of heaven with power and great glory. (Matthew 24:30)

Unknown

But of that day and hour knoweth no man, no, not the angels of heaven, but my Father only. (Matthew 24:36)

Minimum Daily Requirements / Spiritual Vitamins

Sunday: A KING BORN Matthew 1:18–2:23

Monday: KING BEGINS WORK Matthew 4:1-25

Tuesday: KING STATES KINGDOM LAWS Matthew 5:1-17, 41-48; 6:19-34

Wednesday: KING AND HIS FOLLOWERS Matthew 10:1-33

Thursday: THE KINGDOM MYSTERIES Matthew 13:1-52

Friday: THE KING OFFERS HIMSELF AS KING Matthew 21:1-11

Saturday: THE KING WILL RETURN Matthew 25:14-16

Chapter 3

LET'S LOOK AT MARK

MARK PORTRAYS JESUS CHRIST,
THE SERVANT OF GOD

When we speak of a servant, we do not necessarily mean one who only does menial tasks. A servant is one who serves. Christ said, *Let him who would be greatest among you be servant of all.* In this sense the President of the United States is the servant of this great country. He is the greatest citizen because he serves the greatest number. Christ said, *I came not to be ministered unto, but to minister, and to give my life a ransom for many.*

THE SERVANT PREPARED (Read Mark 1:1-13)

We are starting the study of a life that has fascinated men for 2000 years. All these centuries men have studied it and marvelled at it. Jesus the Servant of Jehovah, is on the threshold of His earthly mission, proclaiming the Kingdom of God. He must be prepared for His task. Mark is careful in describing this.

JESUS' PREPARATION

This Gospel begins with John the Baptist. This strange man appears on the scene in an almost sensational way, clothed like the prophets of old in "raiment of camel's hair, and a leathern girdle about his loins." His food, too, was strange, for "locusts and wild honey" were his diet.

There is a lesson here for us. God does not always choose the kind of men we would select. He often picks "the foolish things" to confound the "wise," and the "weak things" to confound the "things which are mighty." (See I Cor. 1:27,28.) No doubt, if we were left to select a herald for Christ, we would have chosen one of high birth, university trained, a man of wide reputation. He would have to be eloquent and a fearless champion of great causes. Not so with God. Graduated from no outstanding school, of humble birth, little known, dressed like a desert hermit, John the Baptist was approved of God. Jesus said of him, *Among them that are born of women there hath not risen a greater than John the Baptist* (Matthew 11:11).

Jesus was baptized with John's baptism in obedience to an appointed ordinance. *Thus it becometh us to fulfill all righteousness* (Matthew 3:15).

Christ was the standard and example of righteousness. He would fulfill every duty He required of others. (I Cor. 10:13)

Jesus was prepared for service by receiving the Holy Spirit *And straightway coming up out of the water, he saw the heavens opened, and the Spirit like a dove descending upon Him* (Mark 1:10).

Mark says, *Immediately* [straightway] *the Spirit driveth Him into the wilderness,* which shows how quickly the Spirit moves. (Mark 1:12) "And" indicated continuity, showing that temptation was as much a part of the preparation of the Servant for His work, as His baptism. Temptation has its place in this world. We could never develop without it. There is nothing wrong in being tempted. The wrong begins when we begin to consent to it. We are not to run into temptation of our own accord. Jesus did not go of Himself, but was led of the Spirit. We will find that the path of duty often takes us through temptations but *God is faithful, who will not suffer you to be tempted above that ye are able; but will with the temptation also make a way to escape, that ye may be able to bear it.* He always makes a way of escape!

THE SERVANT WORKING (Read Mark 1:14—8:30)

Listen to Jesus as He said, *Come ye after me.* (Mark 1:17) What right had an ordinary Nazarene to stop and ask these successful fishermen to come after Him, to leave their business, sit at His feet and not only be His disciples but His servants? Could any one but a king, or emperor, make this demand? Evidently in His voice they heard God's voice.

It is interesting to note that Jesus never called any man from idleness. He called busy and successful men to follow Him. Everyone can turn his business into a channel of service for Christ. How was Christ's call received? *Straightway they forsook their nets and followed Him* (Mark 1:18). Too often there is lost time between our call and our coming. Our doing lags far behind our duty.

Mark records a wonderful statement concerning the Sabbath, in 2:27, *The sabbath was made for man, and not man for the sabbath.* This great saying of Jesus' is the central principle of Sabbath observance. Try spending one Lord's day as Jesus did. I believe you will like it, and I know the Lord will be pleased.

The Servant is always found "working." *I must work the works of Him that sent me, while it is day,* are His words. Read this memorandum of the full days of our Lord's ministry. How empty our own lives will seem in comparison!

The morning following the great Sabbath day of preaching and healing, in which we followed Jesus, He arose very early and went out of the city to a lonely place and prayed. (Mark 1:35) His work was growing rapidly, and Jesus needed heavenly communion. If the Son of God needed to pray before He undertook His work, how much more should we pray. Perhaps our lack of success in life is because we fail at this point. *Ye have not because ye ask not.*

"After some days . . . it was noticed that He was in the house." (Mark 2:1) It is remarkable how rapidly

---

A PERFECT SERVANT'S SABBATH DAY

"How shall I keep the Lord's day?" Jesus did it this way.

He went to church: (Mark 1:21) Even though He, as no other, could see the beauties of nature and remember that He made them all, yet He showed there is value in public worship with others, which no communion with nature can give.

He took part in the services as He had opportunity. (Mark 1:21)

He spent some time in the home of His friend (Peter). (Mark 1:29-31)

He did good to others—works of mercy and love. (Mark 1:32-34)

news spread in the East, without newspapers, railroads, telephones, television or radio. But in another part of the city a man sick with the palsy had heard of this new Prophet and His gospel of healing. His four friends brought him to Jesus and let him down into the presence of the Master. We find in this healing the test and proof of Jesus' power not only as a physician of the body but as a healer of the soul. *Who can forgive sins but God only?* (Mark 2:7) Sins are against God and therefore He only can forgive. Jesus said, *That ye may know that the Son of man hath power on earth to forgive sins, . . . I say unto thee, Arise, and take up thy bed. . .* (See Mark 2:9-12.)

We find the account of the choosing of the twelve in Mark 3:13-21. Notice the fourteenth verse. It tells why Jesus chose these men, *that they should be with Him.* Mark it in your Bible. This is what Jesus wants of His disciples today—that they will take time to be in His presence and commune with Him. In John 15:15, He says, *I call you not servants; . . . but I have called you friends.*

The miracle recorded in Mark 5, like all others, tested the character of men. It took them off their guard and disclosed their true natures. Notice the contrast in the way men received the work of Christ. (vs. 15,17)

It is so with men today. Either men ask Jesus to "depart" because they want to keep their sin, or they ask that He might remain "with" them because they want to lose their sin. Do you want to keep or lose your sin? If Christ stays, sin goes; if sin stays, Christ goes. Be honest!

We must hasten if we would follow this mighty Servant, this Workman of God. Jesus had gone apart in a desert to rest awhile (6:31) but the multitudes followed Him. The feeding of the 5,000 follows without an interval. (Mark 6:32-44) This is one of the most important miracles. Evidently it made a special impression upon the writers of the Gospels, as it is the only one of the thirty-five miracles that is recorded by all.

Peter's confession of faith should be mastered by everyone. (Mark 8:29) Jesus does not tell His disciples who He is. He waits until they tell Him. When He asked, *Whom say ye that I am?* the climax of His ministry was reached. He was testing the aim of all His training of the chosen twelve. Peter's answer gave Him the assurance that His goal had been attained.

What would your answer be if anyone asked you, "What think ye of Christ?" What we think of Christ determines life here and hereafter. Do you think of Him as just a teacher or a prophet? Or can you say with Peter, *Thou art the Christ!*

What Think Ye of Christ?

What did the Pharisees think of Jesus? Already they had agreed to put Him to death.

What did the multitude think of Him? They were deserting Him.

What did the disciples think of Him? Peter gives the answer.

What do you think of Christ?

THE SERVANT REJECTED (Read Mark 8:31—15:47)

Jesus claimed the Kingdom by presenting Himself as the Heir of David, at Jerusalem, according to the prophecy of Zechariah 9:9. (See Mark 11:1-11.)

How did the people accept this King? At first they welcomed Him, because they hoped that He might deliver them from the yoke of Rome and free them from the poverty they were enduring. But when He entered the temple and showed that His mission was a spiritual one, He was hated by the religious leaders with a satanic hatred that led to the plot to put Him to death. (Mark 14:1)

The greatest sin of this age, as of every age, is the rejection of Jesus Christ. Yet, remember that everyone who has heard the Gospel must either accept the Lord as Saviour, or trample Him under foot. The people of Jesus' day made their choice and the people of our day must make theirs.

To believe Christ means life.

To reject Christ means condemnation.

What is Jesus to you? A name? or your Master? If you cannot answer the question as Peter did, will you not sign this covenant, worded by Dr. Torrey?

"I promise to examine carefully the evidence that the Bible is God's Book, and Jesus Christ is God's Son and man's Saviour; and if I find reason to believe that this Book is true and He is man's Saviour, I will accept Him and confess Him before men, and undertake to follow Him."

(Signed)...

The plotting of the chief priests, how they might take Him by craft and put Him to death, and the anointing of His "Body to the burying" by His friends, opens chapter 14. Then the ever sad story of His betrayal at the hand of His own disciple (Mark 14:10,11), the celebration of the Passover and the institution of the Lord's Supper all are crowded into twenty-five short verses. Adding insult to injury, we read of the denial of his Lord by Peter. (Mark 14:26-31, 66-71)

Isaiah's great message is that the Son of God shall become the Servant of God in order that He might die to redeem the world. Mark records how the sufferings of Jesus in Gethsemane and on Calvary only fulfilled the prophecies of Isaiah. (Read Isaiah 53.)

For even the Son of man came not to be ministered unto, but to minister, and to give His life a ransom for many (Mark 10:45).

Jesus was sold for thirty pieces of silver, the price of a slave. He was executed as only slaves were! Yes, Christ was the suffering Servant and died for me! He bore my sins in His own body on the tree.

No reference is made by Mark that in the garden He had the right to summon twelve legions of angels, if He so willed. No promise of the Kingdom is given to the dying thief on the cross. These claims are made by a King (in Matthew), but they are not mentioned by a Servant (in Mark).

THE SERVANT EXALTED (Read Mark 16:1-20)

After the Servant had given His life a ransom for many, He arose from the dead. We read again the great commission (Mark 16:15), also recorded in Matthew 28:19,20. Compare the two. In Mark, we do not hear a King say, *All power is given unto me in heaven and in earth,* as in Matthew. In Mark, we see in Jesus' words that His disciples are to take His place, and He will serve in and through them. He is yet the Worker, though risen. (Mark 16:20) The command rings with urgency of service. Not a corner of the world is to be left unvisited; not a soul to be left out!

Finally He was received into heaven, to sit on the right hand of God. (Mark 16:19) He who had taken upon Himself the form of a servant, is now highly exalted. (See Philippians 2:7-9.) He is in the place of power, ever making intercession for us. He is our advocate.

But Christ is with us. The Servant is always working in us and through us. We are laborers together with Him. (See I Cor. 3:9.) He is still "working with us." (Mark 16:20)

Let us, being redeemed, follow our Pattern, and go forth to serve also!

Therefore, my beloved brethren, be ye steadfast,

unmoveable, always abounding in the work of the Lord, forasmuch as ye know that your labor is not in vain in the Lord (I Cor. 15:58).

Minimum Daily Requirements / Spiritual Vitamins

Sunday: THE SERVANT'S COMING AND TESTING Mark 1:1-20

Monday: THE SERVANT WORKING Mark 2:1–3:25

Tuesday: THE SERVANT SPEAKING Mark 4:1–6:13

Wednesday: THE SERVANT'S MIRACLES Mark 6:32–8:26

Thursday: THE SERVANT'S REVELATION Mark 8:27–10:34

Friday: THE SERVANT'S REJECTION Mark 11:1–12:44

Saturday: THE SERVANT'S DEATH AND TRIUMPH Mark 14:1–16:20

Chapter 4

LET'S LOOK AT LUKE

*LUKE PORTRAYS JESUS CHRIST,
THE SON OF MAN*

The writer of this third Gospel was Dr Luke, Paul's companion. (Acts 16:10-24; II Timothy 4:11; Col. 4:14) He was a native of Syria and apparently was not a Jew, for Colossians 4:14 places him with the other Gentile Christians. If this is true, he was the only Gentile writer of the New Testament books.

PURPOSE

Matthew presents Christ as King, to the Jews.
Mark as the Servant of Jehovah, to the Romans.
Luke as the perfect Man, to the Greeks.
We can never understand how Christ was both God and man, and we never shall, no matter how much we

study God's revelations. When Mr. Webster was asked if he comprehended Christ's deity and humanity, he replied, "No, sir, I cannot; and I should be ashamed to acknowledge Him as my Saviour if I could. If I could comprehend Him, He could be no greater than myself, and I need a superhuman Saviour."

A missionary to the West Indies wanted to bring God and His love to the slaves, but they were toiling all day and he could not get near them. So he sold himself as a slave and worked among them, toiling in the fields, that he might tell them of God's love. This is what Christ did.

THE PREPARATION OF THE SON OF MAN
(Read Luke 1:1–4:13)

The opening of this beautiful book is significant. We learn all about the circumstances that accompanied the birth and childhood of the Holy Babe, and about the one who was sent as His forerunner. The birth of John the Baptist (1:57-80), the angels' song to the shepherds (2:8-20), the circumcision (2:21), the presentation in the temple (2:22-38), and then the story of the boy Jesus, twelve years of age (2:41-52), are all recorded here.

God brings to pass what the prophets have spoken. Micah said that Bethlehem was to be the birthplace of Jesus (Micah 5:2-5), for He was of the family of David. But Mary lived in Nazareth, a town one hundred miles away. God saw to it that Imperial Rome sent forth a decree to compel Mary and Joseph to go to Bethlehem, just as the Child was to be born. Isn't it wonderful how God uses the decree of a pagan monarch, Caesar Augustus, as an instrument to bring to pass His prophecies! God still moves the hand of rulers to do His bidding.

Now look on! We hear the message of the angels to the watching shepherds, but we do not find the wise

men of the East asking for One *who is born King.*
(Luke 2:10-12).

The *Child grew* and *the grace of God was upon Him*
(Luke 2:40). When He was twelve years old, He went
up with His parents to Jerusalem to the feast. He was
found *sitting in the midst of the doctors, both hearing
them, and asking them questions* (Luke 2:46). We find
Jesus' first words were: *Wist ye not that I must be about
my Father's business?* It is the first self-witness to His
deity and to His relationship with the Father. *And they
understood not the saying.*

Again we read, *He went down with them, and came
to Nazareth, and was subject unto them*—these earthly
parents. (Luke 2:51) *Jesus increased in wisdom and
stature, and in favour with God and man* (See Luke
8:42-52). All of these things are peculiar to Jesus as
man, and Luke alone records them. It is important that
we notice Jesus was a "favorite" in Nazareth. It is not a
sign that we are in the grace of God when we are out
of favor with man.

The genealogy of Jesus in Luke is given at the time
of His baptism, and not at His birth. (Luke 3:23)
There are noticeable differences between the genealogy
in Luke and that found in Matthew 1. Won't you take a
few minutes to clear this in your mind?

In Matthew, we have the royal genealogy of the Son
of David, through Joseph.

In Luke, it is His strictly personal genealogy, through
Mary.

*And Jesus being full of the Holy Ghost returned
from Jordan, and was led by the Spirit into the
wilderness, being forty days tempted of the devil* (Luke
4:1, 2).

As Jesus came forth from the fire of testing in the
unabated "power of the Spirit" so can we. It is only as
we are filled with His Spirit that we can overcome

temptation with the power of the Spirit. Everyone snared by temptation, who has lost all hope in himself, can look up to Christ and hear Him say, *Out of every temptation I will make a way to escape, that you may be able to bear it* (See I Cor. 10:13).

The purpose of the temptation was not to discover whether or not Jesus would yield to Satan, but to demonstrate that He could not; to show forth the fact that there was nothing in Him to which Satan could appeal. Christ could be tried and proven.

An automobile salesman wants the prospective buyer to take the car and test it out for himself, not because he fears it will not stand up, but rather because he knows it will.

As you follow Christ in His temptation in the wilderness and study how He overcame His adversary with the *sword of the Spirit,* no doubt there is a greater desire in your own heart to possess this "sword" yourself. There are multitudes of Mohammedan school boys who can quote 6,000 verses of the Koran and can write every word of them from memory. How sad that we Christians have hid so little of the Word of God in our hearts! *Thy Word have I hid in mine heart, that I might not sin against Thee* (Psalm 119:11).

THE MINISTRY OF THE SON OF MAN
(Read Luke 4:14–19:48)

Following the temptation, *Jesus came to Nazareth, where He had been brought up: and, as His custom was, He went into the synagogue on the sabbath day, and stood up for to read* (Luke 4:16). He went to the place where He had been "brought up." Bringing up is an important thing in life. We find that Jesus was accustomed to go to church on the Sabbath day. He had been reared in a godly home. Honestly consider what kind of habits you are forming in your Christian life. How do you spend your Sundays?

Jesus here stated that God had anointed Him to preach deliverance to captives, and bring good tidings to the poor and brokenhearted. (Luke 4:18,19)

Early in Jesus' ministry we see those of His own home town determining to kill Him. (Luke 4:28-30) This is the first hint of His coming rejection. He proclaimed Himself to be the Messiah. (Luke 4:21) They were angered that He should hint that their Jewish Messiah would also be sent to the Gentiles. (See Luke 4:24-30.) They believed God's grace was to be confined to the Jews, and so they were ready to kill Him. He refused to work miracles for them, because of their unbelief. They attempted to cast Him down the brow of the hill, but He escaped to Capernaum. (Luke 4:29-31)

The Jews hated the Gentiles for their treatment of them when they were captives in Babylon. They regarded them with contempt. They considered them unclean and enemies of God. Luke pictures Jesus as tearing down these barriers between Jew and Gentile, saying *that repentance and remission of sins should be preached in His name among all nations, beginning at Jerusalem* (Luke 24:47). The religion of Jesus Christ is not just one of the religions of the world. It is the great world religion, adapted to all nations and to all classes. Read Paul's statement in Romans 1:16.

When the twelve are commissioned (Luke 9), we see a broad field of ministry given. In Matthew we hear the Lord saying, *Go not into the way of the Gentiles, but go rather to the lost sheep of the house of Israel.* Luke omits this and says, *He sent them to preach,* and that *they departed, . . . preaching the gospel everywhere* (Luke 9:2,6).

Wherever this Man, Christ Jesus, went a whole multitude followed Him and *sought to touch Him: for there went virtue out of Him, and healed them all.*

(Luke 6:19) He gave of Himself. Our service must be of this kind. We must give ourselves if we would bind up broken hearts and minister to others.

Gypsy Smith was asked if he would speak at a certain city, and was assured that it would "not take anything out" of him. "It's not worth my going," he replied, "if it doesn't take something out of me." A candle is a perfect type of this sort of Christian service; it cannot give light unless it gives itself.

THE SUFFERING OF THE SON OF MAN
(Read Luke 20:1–23:56)

We have presented in this scene the suffering and death of the Son of Man. It is hard to describe it. How can we understand it? Luke differs from Matthew and Mark in his description.

Jesus is sitting with His disciples, around the table, celebrating the feast of the Passover. At this time He institutes what we call the "Lord's Supper." Listen to His words: *My body which is given for you . . . my blood, which is shed for you.* (Luke 22:19,20) This is different from the account in Matthew and Mark. They say, *My blood which is shed for many.* His love is expressed in such a personal way in Luke. The evangelist adds: *This do in remembrance of Me.* Jesus would be in the minds and hearts of His disciples.

Look into the Garden of Gethsemane. Jesus is praying and "as it were," great drops of blood were on that holy brow. Luke tells us that the angels came to minister to Him, the Son of Man. Matthew and Mark omit this.

In the shadow of the garden, a band of soldiers were approaching; leading them was Judas. But the Scriptures had said that Jesus would be betrayed by a friend, and sold for thirty pieces of silver. (Luke 22:47-62; Psalm 41:9)

Worst of all, His friends deserted Him. Peter denied Him, and all forsook Him and fled except John, the beloved. Luke alone tells us that Jesus looked on Peter, the denier, and broke his heart with that look of love.

We can hardly bear to read of the cruel treatment accorded this God-Man. *For the Son of man is come to seek and to save that which was lost,* (Luke 19:10) but *He came unto His own, and His own* [the Jews] *received Him not.* (John 1:11) (See Luke 22:63-71.)

We follow Jesus into Pilate's hall; then before Herod. (Luke 23:1-12) We follow along the Via Dolorosa to the cross. (Luke 23:27-38) Luke only gives the name Calvary, which is the Gentile name for Golgotha. Luke omits much which Matthew and Mark record, but he alone gives the prayer, *Father, forgive them; for they know not what they do.* And His last words, *Father, into thy hands I commend my spirit* (Luke 23:13-46).

There were three crosses on Calvary's hill. On one of them was a thief, dying for his crimes. Luke tells us this story, too. (Luke 23:39-45) The way this thief was saved is the way every sinner must be saved. He believed on the Lamb of God, who died on the cross that day, to pay the penalty of sin.

The scene closes with the Son of Man crying with a loud voice, *Father into thy hands I commend my spirit.* The centurion, in keeping with this Gospel bears this witness, *Certainly this was a righteous man.*

THE VICTORY OF THE SON OF MAN
(Read Luke 24:1-53)

We turn with great relief from the sorrow and death of the cross, the darkness and gloom of the tomb, to the brightness and glory of the resurrection morning.

Is there any other picture more stirring than this one of the empty tomb? Jesus rose from the dead, and if He arose then shall we rise also. (I Corinthians 15) Look at the picture in Luke 24:1-12.

Luke gives us a part of the scene that the others leave untold. It is the delightful story of the walk to Emmaus.

He shows these disciples that, as their resurrected Lord, He is just the same loving, understanding friend that He had been before His death. After His walk and conversation with them, we hear these disciples urging Him to come in and spend the night with them. He revealed who He was when He lifted up those hands with the wounds, and broke the bread. Then they knew Him, but He vanished out of their sight. On returning to Jerusalem they found abundant proof of the resurrection. He proved that He was a real man with flesh and bones. These details belong to the Gospel of His Manhood, Luke.

Three times His disciples touched Him after He arose. (Matthew 28:9; Luke 24:39; John 20:27) He ate with them, too. (Luke 24:42; John 21:12,13)

As Jesus put out His hand to bless them, He *was carried up into heaven* (Luke 24:51). The fact that He was "carried up" reveals again that He was a man.

He is no longer a local Christ, confined to Jerusalem, but He is a universal Christ. He could say to His disciples, who mourned for Him, thinking when gone He could be no more with them, *Lo, I am with you alway, even unto the end of the age.*

How different now was the hope and joy of those chosen followers, from their despair and shame at the crucifixion! They return to Jerusalem with great joy, and *are continually in the temple, praising and blessing God!*

Minimum Daily Requirements / Spiritual Vitamins

Sunday: THE MAN "MADE LIKE UNTO HIS BRETHREN"
Luke 1:1–3:38

Monday: THE MAN "TEMPTED AS WE ARE" Luke
4:1–8:3

Tuesday: THE MAN "TOUCHED WITH . . . OUR INFIRMI-
TIES" Luke 8:4–12:48

Wednesday: THE MAN "ABOUT MY FATHER'S BUSINESS"
Luke 12:49–16:31

Thursday: THE MAN "NEVER MAN SPAKE LIKE THIS
MAN" Luke 17:1–19:27

Friday: THE MAN, OUR KINSMAN-REDEEMER Luke
19:28–23:56

Saturday: THE MAN IN RESURRECTION GLORY Luke
24:1-53

Chapter 5

LET'S LOOK AT JOHN

JOHN PORTRAYS JESUS CHRIST,
THE SON OF GOD

We open the Book of John with the question in mind: "What do you think of Jesus Christ?" Is He the world's greatest teacher, or is He the true God? Was He one of the prophets, or is He the world's Saviour whose coming was foretold by the prophets?

John purposes to answer these questions once and for all.

Seven Witnesses

The Book of John was written that men might believe

that Jesus Christ is God. John brings seven witnesses to the stand to prove this fact. Here they are.

What do you say, John the Baptist?
This is the Son of God (1:34).

What is your conclusion, Nathanael?
Thou art the Son of God (1:49).

What do you know, Peter?
Thou art that Christ, the Son of the living God (6:69).

What do you think, Martha?
Thou art the Christ, the Son of God (11:27).

What is your verdict, Thomas?
He is *my Lord and my God* (20:28).

What is your statement, John?
Jesus is the Christ, the Son of God (20:31).

What do you say of yourself, Christ?
I am the Son of God (10:36).

Seven Miracles

We find seven signs or miracles, which prove that He is God. *For no man can do these miracles that Thou doest, except God be with him,* were Nicodemus' words. (John 3:2)

Turning water into wine	2:1-11
Healing the nobleman's son	4:46-54
Healing the man at Bethesda	5:1-47
Feeding the 5,000	6:1-14
Walking on the water	6:15-21
Healing the blind man	9:1-41
Raising of Lazarus	11:1-57

Seven "I Am's"

There is another proof of His deity running through

John. He reveals His God-nature in the "I AM's" of this book. He says:

METHODS OF REACHING OTHERS FOR CHRIST

Preaching

John 1:35-51. Andrew heard John the Baptist preach. (1:40)

Testimony of a brother

Andrew told his brother Peter. This is one of the hardest things to do—witnessing in the family circle. (1:41) Try it!

Direct call of Christ

Philip heard Christ's claim and followed. (1:43)

Witness of a friend

Philip aroused Nathanael's interest by saying, Come and see. (1:46) This reminds us how much our personal influence can count.

The scene in John does not open at the manger in Bethlehem, but before all worlds were formed: *In the beginning*. Jesus was the Son of God before "He became flesh and dwelt among us." *In the beginning was the Word*. How like Genesis this book opens!

Christ became what He was not previously—a man. But Christ did not cease to be God. He was God-Man. He lived in a tabernacle of flesh here in this world for 33 years. Incarnation comes from two Latin words, "in" meaning "in," and "caro" meaning "flesh." So Christ was God in the flesh.

Dr. S. D. Gordon tells the story of a mother who was consoling her little daughter, frightened by a storm. "God will take care of you, dear," she said as she tucked her in bed. But the fierce flashing and the awful thundering brought an outcry for her mother. The mother comforted the frightened child and said gently, "You know, dear, I told you God is right here and He will take care of you." The little girl replied, "Yes mother, but you know when it thunders like that a little girl wants somebody with skin on." She longed for the human presence, the warm human touch, and the gentle human voice. Is this not what God did? Jesus was God, coming to us "with skin on"—yes, in the flesh. He came to touch men and to be touched, too, with the feeling of their infirmities.

How was Christ the Word received? Read John 1:11. He came to His own (the Jews) and they received Him not. Imagine a father returning from a long trip and coming to his own house and finding the door locked and the family inside refusing to let him in. It is hard even to picture such a thing. But this is just what happened to Jesus. He presented Himself as King to His people, but He was rejected. All through the book we see Jesus dividing the crowds. As He comes out and speaks the truth, the crowds listen. Some believe and some reject. Christ always divides a crowd even today. *He came unto His own, and His own received Him not.* Tragedy indeed! But not all rejected Him. John presents the results of faith.

THE WAY OF SALVATION

What We Must Do for Salvation:

But as many as received Him, to them gave He power

to become the sons of God, even to them that believe on His name. (John 1:12)

WHAT TO DO: *Believe* and *receive*.

RESULT: You become a child of God.

What Not to Count on for Salvation:

Sometimes the way to better understand what a thing is, is to find out what it is not. In John 1:13, John tells us what salvation is not. *Which were born, not of blood, nor will of the flesh, nor of the will of man, but of God.* All of these things are what people are counting on today for eternal life. The "new birth" makes us "sons of God."

Not of blood—heredity. How much we depend on good birth!

Not of the will of the flesh—culture and education. It is not what we know but Whom we believe that saves us.

Not of the will of man—prestige or influence.

But of God—by the power of the Holy Spirit of God. God comes down and redeems us, if we will only believe and receive Him as Saviour and Lord.

Let us study this Gospel with John's purpose clearly in mind. Read it over again, in John 20:31.

PUBLIC MINISTRY—"AND AM COME INTO THE WORLD" (Read John 1-19–12:50)

Of the seven great witnesses of Christ's deity (that Christ was God), John the Baptist was first. *Behold the Lamb of God!* When at Jesus' baptism, John saw the Spirit descending and remaining on Him, he added, *I saw, and bare record that this is the Son of God.* (1:34) And his final witness is: *This is the Son of God.* (1:34)

In the very beginning, Christ revealed Himself as the Son of God by His words and deeds. The first sign of His deity was the act of turning water into wine. (2:1-11) He merely spoke and it was so. This miracle convinced His disciples that He was the Messiah.

When the rulers asked for a "sign" to prove His authority when Jesus cleansed the temple and drove out the money-changers, He said, *Destroy this temple, and in three days I will raise it up*. The rulers were shocked, for it had taken forty-six years to build this edifice. But *He spake of the temple of His body*, John explains. (2:19-22) The supreme proof of Christ's deity is the resurrection. Read Romans 10:9,10. Have you put your faith in a living Christ?

Jesus gave to this one man the wonderful teachings about eternal life and His love (John 3:16), and the new birth (John 3:6). Nicodemus was a moral, upright man yet Christ said to him, *Ye must be born again*. If Jesus had said this to the woman of Samaria, Nicodemus would have agreed with Him. She was not a Jew and could not expect anything on the ground of her birth as a Samaritan. But Nicodemus was a Jew by birth and he had a right to expect anything on this ground. But it was to him that Jesus spoke, *You must be born from above*.

Suppose that a man born in Ireland would go to the polls on election day with his neighbor, American born. After his neighbor has voted, he steps up and asks for a ballot. "Where were you born?" he is asked. "Ireland." "Are you naturalized?" "No, not yet." "I'm sorry then, you can't vote." "Why not? You let that man vote and I'm as good as he is. I pay my debts more promptly than he and I'm much better to my wife than he." "I'm sorry, sir, but all that is beside the point. The fact is that you are not a naturalized citizen; therefore you cannot vote."

Christ says, *Ye must be born again* in order to enter the Kingdom of Heaven. Have you been born again?

Like the Jews of his day, Nicodemus knew God's law, but nothing of God's love. He was a moral man. He recognized Jesus as a Teacher, but he did not know Him as a Saviour. This is just what the world does today. They put Jesus at the head of the list of the teachers of the world, but they do not worship Him as very God.

Jesus revealed to the woman at the well the truth of His Messiahship. This story gives us Christ's estimate of a single soul. He brought this immoral woman face to face with Himself and showed her what kind of a life she was leading. Her loose view of marriage is not unlike the view taken today by many people. The Lord did not condemn her, but He revealed to her that He is the only One Who could fulfill her needs. Christ revealed the wonderful truth to her that He is the water of life. He alone can satisfy. The wells of the world bring no satisfaction. Men are trying everything, but they still are unhappy and restless. Did the woman believe Christ? What did she do? Her actions spoke louder than any words could have done. She went back and by her simple testimony brought a whole town to Christ. (4:1-42)

In healing the son of the nobleman, we see the second sign of Christ's deity. During His interview with the centurion, we find Jesus bringing this man to an open confession of Christ as Lord—yes, and his whole household joining with him. (4:46-54)

JESUS' STARTLING CLAIMS

Claims to Be Equal with God:

Calls God *My Father.* (5:17) The Jews knew what He meant. *He made Himself equal with God,* they said. They knew that He claimed God as His Father in a sense in which He is not the Father of any other man.

Claims to Be Light of the World:

I am the light of the world: he that followeth me shall not walk in darkness, but shall have the light of life. (John 8:12)

Claims to Be Eternal with God:

Verily, verily, I say unto you, Before Abraham was, I am. (John 8:58)

This claim of eternity with God was unmistakable. He was either the Son of God or a deceiver. No wonder the Jews *took up stones to cast at Him.*

The miracle of the feeding of the 5,000 was an acted parable. Jesus Himself was the Bread from heaven. He wanted to tell them that to all who put their trust in Him will He give satisfaction and joy. (6:35)

The people wanted to make Christ their King because He could feed them. How like men today! They long for someone who can give them food and clothing. Christ says, *Seek ye first the kingdom of God, and His righteousness; and all these things shall be added unto you.* (Matt. 6:33) Christ would not be King on their grounds. He dismissed the excited multitude and departed into a mountain. Men were disappointed that He would not be a political leader, and so they *walked no more with Him.* (John 6:66)

The people were divided because of Jesus. (7:40-44) We find unbelief was developing into actual hostility, but faith was growing in His true followers. Some said, *He is a good man.* Others said, *Not so, but He leadeth the multitude astray.* Men must say one or the other today, when facing Christ's claims. Either He is God, or an impostor. There is no middle ground. What do you say of Christ?

The raising of Lazarus is the final "sign" of John's Gospel. The other Gospel records give the raising of Jarius' daughter and the son of the widow of Nain. But in this case Lazarus had been dead four days. In reality, would it be any harder for God to raise one than the other? Nevertheless it had a profound effect upon the leaders. (11:47,48) The great claim which Jesus made for Himself to Martha is recorded here: *I am the resurrection, and the life: he that believeth in me, though he were dead, yet shall he live: And whosoever liveth and believeth in me shall never die. Believest thou this?* (John 11:25, 26)

This scene closes with Jesus' triumphant entry into Jerusalem. His public ministry has come to an end. It is recorded that many of the chief rulers believed on Him, without making an open confession.

PRIVATE MINISTRY—"AND AM COME INTO THE WORLD" (Read John 13–17)

The Jews had rejected Jesus completely. Now He gathered His own around Him, and told them many secrets before He departed from them. He wanted to comfort His disciples, for He knew how hard it would be for them when He was gone. They would be sheep without a shepherd. This little band was "His own," although they were a feeble lot. His last words before His death are recorded in chapters 13 to 17. It is called the Holy of Holies of the Scriptures.

It is wonderful that Jesus should have selected and loved men like these. They seem to be a collection of "nobodies," with the exception of Peter and John. But they were "His own," and He loved them. One of Jesus' specialties is to make "somebodies" out of "nobodies." This is what He did with His first group of followers, and this is what He has continued to do, down through the centuries. Lincoln said he knew God must love common people because He made so many of them.

After announcing His going, the Lord gives His disciples "a new commandment," that "they love one another." *By this shall all men know that ye are my disciples.* Discipleship is tested not by the creed you recite; not by the hymns you sing; not by the ritual you observe but by the fact that you love one another. The measure in which Christians love one another is the measure in which the world believes in them or their Christ. It is the final test of discipleship. He mentions this "new commandment" again in John 15:12.

Jesus had spoken of His Father, but now He speaks of the other Person of the Godhead, the Holy Spirit. If He (Christ) is to go away, He will send the Comforter, and He will abide with them. This is a wonderful promise for the child of God! Jesus repeats the promise in chapter 15 and again in 16. Look them up. (15:26; chap. 16) Few know of this Presence in their lives. It is by His power that we live. Never call the Holy Spirit "it." He is a Person. He is One of the Godhead.

Jesus reveals the real secret of the Christian life to His disciples in John 15. Abide in Christ. He is the source of life. Abide in Christ as the branch abides in the vine. The branch cannot sever itself and join itself whenever it will, to the trunk. It must abide if it will bear fruit. This is the picture of our lives in Christ. Live and walk in Christ, and you will bear fruit. If you are not abiding in Christ, the fruit will soon disappear. As the branch without the vine is dead, so are we without Christ. A light bulb may be perfect, but if it is not in full contact with the current it will not burn. This, too, is the picture of abiding in the place of power.

After He ended His talk with the eleven disciples, Jesus spoke to the Father. The disciples listened to His loving and solemn words. How thrilled they must have been as He told the Father how much He loved them, and how He cared for them! If you would know the beauty and depth of these wonderful words, kneel in prayer and let Jesus lead you as you pray and read John 17.

SUFFERING AND DEATH—"AGAIN, I LEAVE THE WORLD" (Read John 18; 19)

"The hour" had come! The greatest work of Christ on earth remained to be done. He was to die, that He might glorify the Father and save a sinful world. He came to give His life a ransom for many. Christ came into the world by a manger and left it by the door of the cross.

All the disciples but John deserted Jesus in the hour of His greatest need. In that fleeing crowd was James of the "inner circle," Nathanael the guileless, and Andrew the personal worker. Yet here they were, running pell-mell down the road together, away from their Friend. A sorry sight! Wait! Don't start blaming them. Suppose you look up and see where you are. Are you following Jesus closely? Remember, majorities aren't always right. Be sure you are right! Can Christ count on you?

The Judas Clan of betrayers have not all died yet.

The Simon Clan of deniers are still with us.

The Fleeing Nine Clan are still here.

The John Clan of the faithful are still few.

Which badge hangs upon the inside wall of your spirit? Answer this question honestly.

At the cross we have hate's record at its worst, and love's record at its best. Man so hated that he put Christ to death. God so loved that He gave men Life.

Our religion is one of four letters, instead of two. Other religions say, "Do." Our religion says, "Done." Our Saviour has done all on the cross. He bore our sins and when He gave up His life, He said, *It is finished!* This was the shout of a conqueror. He had finished man's redemption. Nothing was left for man to do but to believe it. Has the work been done in your heart?

Salvation is costly. *Christ died for our sins.* (I Cor. 15:3) It cost Him His life.

49

An Indian boy saved his little sister, who had been bitten by a rattlesnake, by placing his lips to the bite and sucking the poison from the wound. But a sore on his own lip meant his death, for the poison spread in his own body. The Lord Jesus Christ heard our cry when we had been bitten by the Old Serpent. He dealt the death blow to our enemy, the Devil, and took the poison of sin for us, and it killed Him.

A doctor lived in a Scotch village. He was noted for his skill and piety. After his death his books were examined and several accounts were found to be marked across in red ink, "Forgiven—too poor to pay." His wife, quite different, said, "These accounts must be paid." She sued for the money. The judge said, "Is this your husband's handwriting in red ink?" She answered, "It is." The judge replied, "Then there is not a court in the land that can obtain money where he has written, 'Forgiven'." Even so, Christ has released us from our spiritual debts, and has written, "Thy sins be forgiven."

VICTORY OVER DEATH—"AND GO TO THE FATHER"
(Read John 20:21)

We have a Saviour who is victorious over death. He "ever liveth."

On the third day the tomb was empty! The grave-clothes were all in order. Jesus had risen from the dead, but not as others had done. When Lazarus came forth, he was bound in his grave-clothes. He came out in his natural body. But when Jesus come forth His natural body was changed to a spiritual body. The changed body came right out of its linen wrappings and left them, as the butterfly leaves the chrysalis shell. Read what John says, in 20:6-8.

Jesus' appearances, ten in all, after His resurrection, helped His disciples to believe that He was God. Read the confession of the seventh witness, Thomas the

Doubter. (John 20:28) *And Thomas answered and said unto Him, My Lord and my God.* Jesus wanted every doubt to be removed from each one of His disciples. They must carry out His great commission and bear the Gospel into the world. (John 20:21)

To Peter, who denied Him thrice, Jesus gave the opportunity of confessing Him thrice. He planned to restore him to full privileges of service again. Christ only wants those who love Him to serve Him. If you love Him, you must serve Him. No one who loves Christ can help but serve.

What are Jesus' last words in this Gospel? "Follow thou Me." This is His word to each one of us. May we all follow Him in loving obedience "till He come"!

Minimum Daily Requirements / Spiritual Vitamins

Sunday: CHRIST BECAME FLESH John 1:1-51

Monday: CHRIST SO LOVED John 3:1-36

Tuesday: CHRIST SATISFIES John 4:1-54

Wednesday: CHRIST, THE BREAD OF LIFE John 6:1-59

Thursday: CHRIST, THE LIGHT OF THE WORLD John 9:1-41

Friday: CHRIST, OUR SHEPHERD John 10:1-39

Saturday: CHRIST PROMISES THE COMFORTER John 14:1-31

Chapter 6

LET'S LOOK AT ACTS

ACTS PORTRAYS JESUS CHRIST,
THE LIVING LORD

Christ had told His disciples that He would send the
Spirit, and *He shall bear witness of me: . . .* This
promise of Christ was fulfilled on the day of Pentecost
when He poured forth the Holy Spirit upon the disciples. (Acts 2:16,17,33)

This book tells of the extension of the Gospel to the
Gentiles. All through the Old Testament we find God
dealing with the Jew. In the New Testament we find
Him working among all nations.

POWER FOR WITNESSING (Read Acts 1; 2)

Our Lord spent a wonderful forty days with His
disciples, after His resurrection. After He had spoken

His last words to them (recorded in Acts 1:8), He was taken up *and a cloud received Him out of their sight.* Think of so great an event told in such a few words! The Father took His Son back to glory. There was no chariot of fire, as when Elijah was taken. No whirlwind was necessary to lift Him to His throne. (See Acts 1:9-11.) Hence, Jesus did not go away. He merely went out of sight. Henceforth He will be an unseen Presence, for He promised, *Lo, I am with you alway.*

This same Jesus . . . shall so come in like manner as ye have seen Him go into heaven. (Acts 1:11) If this is so, we should examine how He went. Then we shall know He will come back. See what the Scriptures say. It will be:

Personal ....I Thess. 4:16
Visible ....Revelation 1:7
Bodily ....Matthew 24:30
Local ....Luke 24:50

Next in importance to the coming of our Lord Jesus Christ to this earth, is the coming of the Holy Spirit. The Church was born on that great day of Pentecost. (Acts 2)

The wonderful thing about Pentecost was not the mighty wind or the tongues of fire, but the disciples' being filled with the Holy Spirit, that they might be witnesses to men. If we do not have the desire to tell others of Christ, it is evident that we do not know the fullness of the Holy Spirit.

Do not think that at Pentecost the Holy Spirit came into the world for the first time. All through the Old Testament we see accounts of His guiding men and giving them strength. Now the Spirit was to use a new instrument, the Church, which had been born on that day.

The theme of this first Christian sermon was that Jesus is the Messiah, as shown by His resurrection.

The real power of the Holy Spirit was shown when Peter, the humble fisherman, rose to speak, and 3,000 souls were saved! How can we account for cowardly Peter's boldness as he stood that day to preach before a multitude on the streets of Jerusalem? What was the secret of Peter's ministry? This is often asked of men. There was only one reason. Peter was filled with the Holy Ghost. Before such a man the multitudes always melt.

It is a serious thing to charge men with murder; yet Peter did just this. (Acts 2:36) Will he get away with it? Will he be stoned? The last verses in chapter 2 answer the question. *Now when they heard this, they were pricked in their heart, and said unto Peter and to the rest of the apostles, Men and brethren, what shall we do?* (Acts 2:37)

What a Church was this First Church of Jerusalem, organized with a membership of 3,000 on the day of Pentecost! What glorious days followed, in "teaching" and "fellowship," and "signs and wonders," and, above all, salvation! *The Lord added to the church daily such as should be saved.* (Acts 2:47) This is the real objective of the Church. Are we seeing it today in our churches?

WITNESSING IN JERUSALEM (Read Acts 3:1–8:3)

Three conflicts disturbed the early Church. (Acts 3–7) The first real opposition grew out of the miracle of Peter's healing the lame man at the Gate Beautiful of the temple. Peter took advantage of the crowd which had gathered around the man, and preached his second recorded sermon. He aroused the leaders because he taught the people that this Jesus, whom they had crucified, was their long-promised Messiah. So powerful were the words of Peter and John that 5,000 men turned to Christ! (Acts 4:4) The rulers forbade the

MEDITERRANEAN LANDS

PAUL'S MISSIONARY JOURNEYS

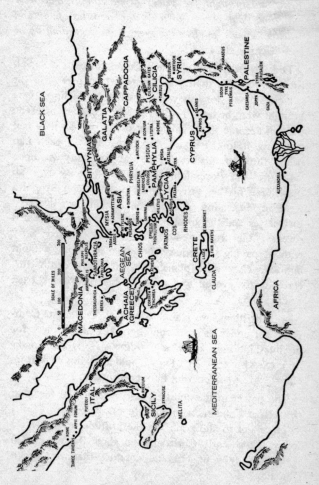

apostles to preach Jesus, but opposition only made the Church thrive. (See Acts 4:18,31.)

Neither was there any among them that lacked: for as many as were possessors of lands or houses sold them, and brought the prices of the things that were sold, and laid them down at the apostles' feet: and distribution was made unto every man according as he had need. (Acts 4:34,35)

Did the early Church teach Communism? Or Socialism? Never! No man was compelled to part with his personal possessions. It was not expected of him. If he brought what he had, it was a purely voluntary act. The Church became so unselfish that many sold all they had and gave it to the apostles to distribute "as each had need." But even this act of love and generosity was open to abuse and deception. Barnabas' liberality was an illustration of the spirit of love. Ananias and Sapphira were an illustration of deception in that they deceived themselves and the apostles as well. But the Holy Spirit revealed the truth about it all. They wanted glory without paying the price. They wanted honor without honesty. They were punished with instant death, for, claiming to give all to God, they had kept back part. (Acts 5:4,5)

As Christians, we claim to give all to Christ. Complete surrender is the condition He sets down for discipleship. *Forsake all and follow Me,* is His condition. (See Luke 14:33.) Do we hold anything back from Christ? Are we hypocrites in our testimony?

The power in the apostles' story was in the fact that their lives fitted in with the life of their risen Christ. "You've got to show me," is the attitude of the world today. Those early Christians did show the world. Do you show by your life and conduct that you are a Christian?

The disciples persisted in preaching the Word. (Read Acts 5:12-42.) The Sadducees who did not believe in the resurrection, were again stirred up by the disciples, continuing to teach the resurrection of Jesus. Although they threw the apostles into prison, God opened the prison doors and brought them forth. (Acts 5:19)

Nothing stopped their mouths. See the result of this second opposition. (Acts 5:41,42) Their statement: *We ought to obey God rather than men,* should be the conviction of every life. Is it yours?

This opposition was centered around Stephen. Read the experiences as recorded in Acts 6 and 7. Stephen was just a layman, but he was one of the first deacons. He is described as *a man full of faith and power.* (Acts 6:8) We have a record of but one day of his life—the last. What an account it is! It is not the length of time we live that counts, but how we live. Someone has said, "A Christian is always on duty." This means that every minute of his life is important and under God's direction.

The leaders in the synagogue *were not able to resist the wisdom and the spirit by which he spake.* Their anger flared into murderous hatred. Stephen was the first martyr of the Christian Church. To Stephen's death we may trace, without doubt, the first impressions made by the followers of Christ on Saul.

WITNESSING IN JUDEA AND SAMARIA
(Read Acts 8:4–12:25)

The disciples had been witnesses in Jerusalem, but Jesus had told them they must go into Judea and Samaria. How was this to be accomplished?

If you were quite sure that you would lose your life by remaining in your own home town, but would be safe in some nearby village, do you think you would go to that village? This is the very problem that faced the early

Church in Jerusalem. There were religious leaders there who thought they were doing God's will when they tried to wipe out Christianity by killing the Christians. Paul said: *I verily thought with myself, that I ought to do many things contrary to the name of Jesus of Nazareth.* (Acts 26:9)

Paul really began his work of spreading the Gospel then but he didn't know it. Read Acts 8:3. He thought he was stamping out Christianity. Instead, he was spreading it. Just laugh when you see anyone opposing Christianity. Persecution always has spread Christianity like wind spreads fire.

This explains the spreading of the work into Samaria. (Acts 8:1) Who was the chosen leader for Samaria? (Acts 8:5) Not Peter, but Philip, one of the deacons. Philip had settled in Samaria. He was an evangelist. Jesus said, *Ye shall be witnesses in . . . Samaria.* Philip preached Christ and his evangelistic campaign was meeting with tremendous success. (See Acts 8:6-8.) But God had another mission for him. He told Philip to leave his growing work and *go toward the south unto the way that goeth down from Jerusalem unto Gaza, which is desert.* (Acts 8:26) Philip met an Ethiopian. "By chance," you say? When you are in the will of God, things do not happen by chance. No friend crosses your path by accident. No joy or sorrow comes into your life except by God's permission.

God teaches us the importance of winning just one person to Christ. If each one kept winning one to Christ every day, and the one he won would do the same, startling things would result. All the millions in the United States could be won in a little over a month! This seems incredible, but it is true. No doubt Philip's convert, the Ethiopian, introduced the Gospel into the great continent of Africa. The Gospel was on the way to the uttermost part of the earth.

It was at Stephen's death that we have the first mention of Saul. Stephen's martyrdom seemed to have inflamed this persecutor of the Church. Saul was struggling with an aroused conscience. He knew he was in the wrong, but he wouldn't give up. That is why Jesus told him in his vision that it was hard for him to kick against the pricks. (Acts 26:14)

Saul made havoc of the Church! The more moral and intelligent a man is, the more harm he can do when controlled by Satan rather than by God. It is not "bad" men who have the worst influence. No one would listen to a man sprawling in the gutter, or take seriously what he says, but everyone respects a man in authority.

The story of Saul's conversion is one of the most thrilling accounts in history. Become familiar with this great story. He was a man *breathing out threatenings and slaughter against the disciples of the Lord.* (Acts 9:1, 2) Then we find him preaching *Christ in the synagogues, that He is the Son of God.* (Acts 9:20)

Every step of his three great missionary journeys Paul made known Christ's will with unmistakable clarity. There is no doubt that Paul holds the most important place of any man in the New Testament. He was converted and made an apostle by Christ Himself. It was to him that Christ gave first hand revelations of truth, and to him Christ committed the doctrine of the Church. To what people was Paul especially sent? He was the Apostle to the Gentiles, as Peter had been to the Jews.

What had Peter done since Pentecost? It is not only what a man believes but what he is doing about it, that counts. Christ had told Peter that he was to be a witness. Peter helped start the first Church, worked miracles, and baptized thousands. His work had been among the Jews.

We find Peter now in the house of Simon the tanner.

(Acts 10:5,6) God was going to show Peter that the Gospel was for the Gentiles as well as the Jews. (Acts 10:9-16) The high wall of religious difference between Jew and Gentile must be broken down. Peter was the man God used to start leveling it. Christ was building a Church and He wanted both Jews and Gentiles to be the living stones of which it is to be formed. (Eph. 2:20-22)

At Pentecost, Peter had used the "keys of the kingdom" entrusted to him, to open the door of the Gospel to the Jews. While Paul was in Tarsus, Peter in the house of Cornelius put the key into the lock of the door that had barred the Gentiles, and opened it. (Acts 10:1-48) Read this account. What about race prejudice today? Do you think that what God told Peter to do was easy? (Acts 10:14-16) What is the Church doing today?

Think where we would have been today if the Gospel had not been for the Gentiles! Suppose Peter had said what so many Christians say today, "O, I am going to work among my own people. There is enough to do at home. Why go to other people?"

Do we realize that we Americans might have been pagans, living in heathen darkness and superstition, while the Chinese and Japanese would have been Christian nations if the first missionaries had gone East instead of coming West? Wouldn't you think that Americans, above every people, ought to believe in missions? Think what our condition might have been today, if missionaries had not brought Christ to us.

WITNESSING IN THE UTTERMOST PART OF THE EARTH (Read Acts 13—28)

The death of Stephen was only the beginning of great persecution of the Christians. How did they ever get to Antioch? (Acts 11:19-21) Someone has called Christianity in the early days, "A Tale of Two Cities"—Jerusalem and Antioch.

Up through Acts 12, we have seen the beginning of the Church, with Peter as its leader, in Jerusalem. From Acts 13 through 28, we are going to see Paul and the Church at Antioch. Antioch is the new base of operations. All the wonderful missionary journeys of Paul started from here, not from Jerusalem. It became the new center of the Church for carrying out Jesus' commission, *unto the uttermost part of the earth.* It was at Antioch that they were first called Christians. (Acts 11:26)

The first great missionary journey soon started with Paul and Barnabas going westward from Antioch. (Acts 13:2,3) The greatest enterprise in the world is foreign missions, and here we see the very beginning of it. The whole idea began just the way it should, in a prayer meeting. Our first missionary society in America was born in a prayer meeting held under a haystack at Williams College.

While Paul and Barnabas were out preaching in the face of persecution and suffering, the Church Council at Jerusalem was trying to answer one of the most troublesome questions. It really was this: "Must a Gentile become a Jew and accept his laws and ceremonies before he can become a Christian?" (Acts 15:1) Paul and Barnabas had said nothing about the law of Moses. They had stated: *Believe on the Lord Jesus Christ, and thou shalt be saved.*

Many today are not just clear in their knowledge of what a person must do to become a Christian. We will never merit salvation, and we will never gain it by any effort on our part, *for by grace are ye saved . . . not of works.* (See Ephesians 2:4-9.) The law doesn't save anyone. It only shows how sinful we are. It is like a mirror. The mirror shows us how we look but does not change our looks.

They came to an important decision in that Church

Council. They found out that God now was going to *take out of them a people for His name.* (See Acts 15:14.) He was going to form His Church of those He called out.

Paul and Barnabas went out on their second missionary tour to visit all the churches they had established and to see how the new Christians were getting along. After a disagreement with Barnabas about John Mark, Paul took Silas, his new found friend, and went through Syria and Cilicia. In Lystra he found Timothy whom he trained to become a preacher of this blessed Gospel. (II Timothy 1:5; Acts 16:1) God often brings about these great human friendships.

The Holy Spirit was Paul's constant Guide. It was at Troas that the Holy Spirit, in a vision, directed Paul to take the Gospel for the first time into Europe. (Acts 16:8-11) The starting point was Philippi in Macedonia. The ship that carried Paul from Asia to Europe, bore the seed of a new civilization and life. It carried the Gospel of the Lord Jesus Christ.

Do you think that Christians are "called" into definite fields of service today? What about the call of the child widow of India, the starving in China, the demon-tortured in Africa? Are they not calling to Christians for relief and instruction and salvation? Paul saw a man calling him, and he answered. There are a billion and a half lost souls in the world today, calling to us. The call comes from every corner of the earth.

Paul's experiences in the greatest cities of his day were crowded with interest. He founded a church in Thessalonica, a rich busy city (Acts 17:4), at Corinth, a very wicked city (Acts 18:8), in Ephesus, the world's most cosmopolitan center outside of Rome. As he traveled, he kept writing his wonderful epistles. We read them today in the New Testament with great profit and interest.

Paul's last missionary journey must have been a heartbreaking experience. He had to say farewell at every place. He knew it was a final farewell. Read Acts 20:37,38. They all wept and fell on Paul's neck, the Oriental expression of sorrow, knowing they would never see him again. Think of this sad experience repeated a dozen times over. Probably no man, except David, has ever inspired such intense personal love in so many hearts. Think of what the love of God was able to do in the heart of a Saul of Tarsus!

Sailing out of the harbor of Ephesus, Paul bids his friends a last farewell. He is headed for Jerusalem, and from now on he is seen as *the prisoner of the Lord*. Paul makes his last visit to Jerusalem and here one of those swiftly formed mobs, which gather so quickly in the excitable Orient, rushed against the apostle and bound him, declaring he was teaching the Jews to forsake Moses. Finding that Paul was a Roman citizen, the chief captain promised to give him a fair trial. Paul made his defense before the Roman governor, Felix, at Caesarea. After two years' imprisonment, Paul was tried a second time, before the new governor, Festus, and appealed from him to Caesar himself, the emperor in Rome. (Acts 21:27–26:32)

After a most exciting voyage, with one ship wrecked in a terrific storm off the coast of Malta, Paul arrived in Rome and was kept a prisoner for another two years, although in his own hired house. Even in prison the great preacher and evangelist led the servants in Nero's own palace to Christ. Service for the Master can brighten life's darkest hours. When we seek to lift other's burdens, we lighten our own. (See Acts 27:1–28:24.)

During his imprisonment, Paul wrote many of his epistles. It was while he was in a dungeon in Rome, expecting at any hour to be beheaded, that he wrote his second epistle to Timothy and said, *I am now ready to be offered, and the time of my departure is at hand. I have fought a good fight, I have finished my course, I have kept the faith:* . . . (II Timothy 4:6-8)

Finally the beloved apostle was condemned and beheaded. His heroic soul was released and the body buried in the catacombs of Rome.

Paul changed Christianity from its Jewish tribal confines to a world-wide influence. He tried to break down the barriers between Jew and Gentile, bond and free.

Are you impressed, student, in the study of the life of this man, by the marvelous things God can do with a life wholly surrendered and Spirit filled?

This is the only unfinished book in the Bible. Notice how abruptly it closes! How else would it close? How could there be a complete account of a Person's life work as long as He lives? Our risen and ascended Lord still lives. From the center, Christ, the lines are seen proceeding in every direction, but *the uttermost part of the earth* is not yet reached. The book marks only the beginning. The Gospel of Christ moves on! You are still living the Acts.

A POD OF P'S

Person of the Book: the Lord Jesus Christ.
Power of the Book: the Holy Spirit.
Preachers of the Book: Peter and Paul.
Places of the Book: Jerusalem and Antioch.
Program of the Book: Missions.

Minimum Daily Requirements / Spiritual Vitamins

Sunday: FIRST CHURCH IN JERUSALEM Acts 1:1–4:37

Monday: WITNESSING IN JERUSALEM Acts 5:1–8:3

Tuesday: WITNESSING IN JUDEA AND SAMARIA Acts 8:4–12:25

Wednesday: PAUL ESTABLISHES THE CHURCHES (FIRST TOUR) Acts 13:1–15:35

Thursday: PAUL REVISITS THE CHURCHES (SECOND TOUR) Acts 15:36–18:21

Friday: PAUL ENCOURAGES THE CHURCHES (THIRD TOUR) Acts 18:22–25:9

Saturday: PAUL SENT TO ROME Acts 25:10–28:31

Chapter 7

LET'S LOOK AT ROMANS

ROMANS PORTRAYS JESUS CHRIST,
OUR RIGHTEOUSNESS

We now begin a study of the Epistles in the New Testament. Thirteen of the twenty-one were written by Paul; hence they are called the Pauline Epistles. He wrote his letters to the churches at Thessalonica, Galatia, Corinth and Rome during his missionary journeys. It was while he was a prisoner in Rome that he wrote his letters to the church at Ephesus, one to the Colossians, one to Philemon and one to the Philippians. After his imprisonment he wrote two letters to Timothy and one to Titus.

The Book of Romans tells us of God's method of making guilty men good.

The key verse of this great thesis is found in Romans 1:16,17. Commit these great verses to memory.

ROMANS IN A NUTSHELL
(Romans 1:16,17)

The Person of the Gospel......................Christ
The Power of the Gospel.................Power of God
The Purpose of the Gospel...............Unto Salvation
The People to whom sent...................To everyone
The Plan of acceptance.......To everyone who believeth
The Particular result..........The just shall live by faith

Paul was proud of the Gospel, because he had proved its power in his own life, and in the lives of all who would believe.

GOD'S NEWS FOR MEN IN A BAD STATE

God's news! These words will command the attention of anyone. Say, "I have good news for you!" and one can always secure a listener. The real value of "good news" depends on the source—who said it. This is why the Gospel Paul presents is so welcome. This news comes from God. Romans is Paul's shout of joy to a lost world. "Eureka! I have found the way! It is Jesus Christ, my Lord!"

In Romans we find an offer of the righteousness of God to the man who finds himself stripped by the law of his own righteousness. The Book of Romans pictures man as a train passenger who has lost his ticket and hasn't a cent to buy another.

WHAT WE ARE BY NATURE
(Read Romans 1:1–3:20)

Why does man need salvation? Because he is a sinner. God has X-rayed the human heart and has given us the picture. He shows us what He finds in us all. The findings are so terrible that they cannot be read in a mixed audience. But remember, this is the picture of us that God sees. I know your picture is there because it says, *There is none that doeth good, no, not one*. This fact Paul proves conclusively in the first three chapters of this Book of Romans. This is the picture of man without God. Read every word of Romans 3. You will believe then that the natural heart is desperately wicked. Have you ever asked the Holy Spirit to throw a searchlight on your own heart? If you have, you know today that you need a Saviour.

When we go to have a photograph taken, we fix ourselves up. Then when the photographer gives us the proofs he assures us that the finished picture will look nothing like them. He removes all the wrinkles and warts and we think they are a splendid likeness. But this is not the kind of a picture God takes. He shows us just what we are.

The Book of Romans presents a courtroom scene. God, the Judge of all the earth, summons Jew and Gentile before the bar of justice. Prisoner after prisoner is brought up.

The general charge is stated—*All Under Sin*. (Romans 3:19) Both the Gentile (2:1-16) and Jew (2:17-3:8) are given the opportunity for a hearing. Their special pleas of "not guilty" are carefully considered and answered, clearing the way for the final verdict from the Judge.

Finally the Judge pronounces the verdict. *All the world . . . guilty before God*. (Romans 3:19,20) If this were today, newspapers everywhere would blaze this headline. All the newsboys would be calling it forth. Can't you hear them? *"ALL — THE — WORLD — FOUND — GUILTY!"*

Do not say, "God is love. He will not condemn me." Listen to God's words here: *The wrath of God is revealed from heaven against all ungodliness.* (Romans

1:18) He has already passed sentence on everyone. "All . . . guilty." There is no chance of appeal. It is the decision of the Supreme Court of the universe. Sin is universal—*All have sinned!* Hence we need a world's Saviour. Because God is a God of love, He has provided just this One! Repeat aloud John 3:16. The Judge on the bench says, "Is there anyone to appear for the prisoners?" Then the Son of God says, "Yes, I am here to represent these. It is true that they committed these sins. It is true that they are guilty, but I bore their guilt on the cross. I died in their place that they might go free. I am their righteousness." And the Judge sets them free.

We get an awful picture of sin in these first three chapters of Romans. Remember, SIN is a marksman's word. It means "missing the mark"—the standard that God has set for us. God's Word says, *All have sinned, and come short*—in our good deeds? No—*of the glory of God.* Do not measure your life by any other standard but this. Do not "compare yourselves among yourselves." Of course you may not have fallen as short as some others you know, but you are "short" as far as God is concerned. Use Christ alone as the measure of righteousness that God demands.

If you would try to gain heaven by climbing to the highest peak of the Rocky Mountains, you still would be far "short" of the distance required. Even man's supreme effort to please God by good deeds and fine gifts falls short. You cannot attain unto the righteousness that God demands, no matter how far you climb. God says, *All come short of the glory.* "All are guilty of death," for *all have sinned.* Only One has spanned the distance from earth to heaven—He is Christ Jesus, our Lord. He is the only Way clear through to God.

We are all sinners because we were born into a sinful race. We are all "sons of Adam." But we were not only born into sin; we have sinned ourselves for *all have sinned*. Remember this—we sin because we are sinners. This is our nature. A plum tree bears plums, because it is a plum tree. The fruit is the result of its nature. Sin is the fruit of a sinful heart. *The heart is deceitful above all things.* (Jeremiah 17:9)

HOW TO BECOME A CHRISTIAN
(Read Romans 3:21–5:21)

God's plan of salvation runs through the entire Scripture. It is like the cordage of the British Navy with a scarlet line interwoven through it that you cannot take out without destroying the cord. There is a scarlet line of salvation running through Scripture. You can see it very plainly in certain portions of the Bible. (Romans 3)

Some simple steps in these next paragraphs will show you "How to become a Christian."

I'm a Sinner!

One does not have to be a sinner in the sight of men to be lost. Of course there is a difference in the degree of sin, but not in the fact of sin, and its results, for *the wages of sin is death*. One may be drowned in seven feet of water and be as dead as if he had been submerged in seventy feet of water. In our inability to save ourselves, we are all on the same level—*There is no difference* (Romans 3:22).

How Can I Be Saved!

We are saved by Christ's righteousness. He has made it available for us by His death. *Being justified freely by His grace through the redemption that is in Christ Jesus:* . . . (Romans 3:24,25).

Christ Died for Me!

I am a person condemned to die because of my sin, for *the wages of sin is death*. But I can look on the cross and see that Christ has already died for me. I believe that He died for my sin. And so in exchange for my poor, sinful, condemned life, I can accept His righteousness and His life. (I Peter. 2:24)

I Accept His Righteousness!

He that believeth on the Son hath everlasting life. (John 3:36) Apart from man's effort to be good, God has provided his righteousness, the Lord Jesus Christ. Our righteousness is as filthy rags. (Romans 3:21,22)

I Have Eternal Life!

Your sin is on Christ. He has borne it for you. Have you accepted Him as your Saviour and *passed from death unto life?* (John 5:24) If you have decided to let Christ be your sin-bearer, you now have His salvation. (Read Romans 3:24)

When God looks at us, He sees no righteousness. (See Romans 3:10.) When God looks at us "in Christ," He does not see an improvement but perfection, for God sees only His own Righteousness, Jesus Christ.

You have become acquainted with one great word of Scripture, "salvation." Here is another—"justification." "Just-as-if-I'd"—Everything that Christ has done has been credited to my account. His righteousness is mine!

When Christ's righteousness is reckoned as ours, this is called "justification"—a man made just before God. *The just shall live by faith.* A man is not made just by his works, but by believing on Christ. (Read Romans 3:28.) This great truth brought the young monk, Martin Luther, to his feet as he was creeping up the holy stairs in Rome, doing penance for his sin. It gave birth to the great Reformation. It freed the believer from the idea that men were saved by works to a life of faith and liberty in Christ. Not only are we saved by faith, but we must live by faith, trusting in Christ.

Paul gives us illustrations of justification by faith from the Old Testament. Especially does he tell us of how Abraham's faith was counted for righteousness. (Romans 4) Abraham received three things by faith: righteousness, inheritance, posterity. (Romans 4:3, 13,17)

We too, have great benefits when we are justified by His grace. Grace is unmerited favor. In this life we find that faith is followed by peace, pardon and promise, (Romans 5:1-5) and more than all, an assurance of our salvation. (Romans 5:6-11)

There is a question that many ask: "How could one man die for the whole world?" One man might take another man's place and be his substitute. That is all right, you say, but for one to die for the whole world—that is nonsense! Let us see if this is true!

None of us likes the idea of being called a "sinner," but we must face what we are. Listen to what Paul says in Romans 5:12-21. We were born sinners. We were not asked if we wished to come into this world. We woke up to the fact one day that we were subject to a sinful nature. Adam, the head of our race, was not created that way. (Genesis 1:26) He deliberately sinned and his sinful nature was passed on to us all. We sin because we are sinners.

But over against Adam, the head of the natural race, we find Christ, the Head of a spiritual race—"a new creation." When I was born in this body, I was born a descendant of Adam. I have his nature which is sinful. When I am born into the family of God, by Christ Jesus, I have Christ's nature which is holy. In the words of Scripture, *As in Adam all die, even so in Christ shall all be made alive.* (I Cor. 15:22) I did not choose to be a descendant of Adam. I may choose to be a child of God. If one man's sin made it possible for all the race to die, one Man's righteousness made it possible for all the race to get out of this condition. (Read Romans 5:15.)

Have you received "eternal life by Jesus our Lord?" Are you a sinner "in Adam," or are you a son "in Christ?"

HOW TO LIVE A CHRISTIAN LIFE
(Read Romans 6–8)

We have learned how to become a Christian. Now we must find out how to live like a Christian.

In Romans 6 there are three important words. Mark them.

KNOW that Christ died for us. (Romans 6:3-5,10) We died with Christ. (Romans 6:8)

RECKON on this! Count on it as true! (Romans 6:11)

If a relative told you that he had put $500 in the bank for you for a trip and you could draw it any time you needed it, you would count on it, I am sure, though you never saw the money. If you should question it, and not draw it out, the money would never be yours. If you reckon it yours by signing a check and passing it through the bank window, that which you have never seen becomes a reality. Reckoning makes things real!

Since we are dead to sin and alive unto God, how shall we live? See Romans 6:13.

YIELD—(Romans 6:13)

This means "let go" of your life and "let God" live through you. This is the surrendered life. This is the right way to live a life of victory and blessing. Let Him work His will in you and through you.

Be like a dog off his leash that at first dashes down the street, enjoying his freedom, but soon comes back to walk demurely beside his master. The spirit of the master holds him. He belongs to him. He needs no chain to bind him.

The Christian soon finds a new standard for his life. He does not try to live up to the Law, for he is no longer under it. He strives to please the One who dwells within him. *For to me to live is Christ,* and *I do all to the glory of God.*

Romans 6 reveals the secret of a life of victory. I am living in Christ! Dead is sin, but alive to God! It tells me how "I" can lead a Christian life. Self, we have learned, was a condemned thing, unable to be good, never righteous. (Romans 3) Now when self becomes a Christian and tries to live a Christian life, it finds this to be impossible. We are saved by faith, and we cannot live by our own efforts.

This sad truth is revealed in Romans 7. It tells us how we cannot live a victorious life. Mark the title word "I" and you will find it is used thirty-eight times in the twenty-five verses of this chapter. The Holy Spirit is never mentioned. Although "I" tries, it finds only defeat and failure.

Dr. Griffith Thomas said, "It is not hard to live a Christian life; it is impossible."

Paul said, *It is not I that live, but Christ that lives in me.*

Listen to the words of the man who tries to live by his own effort. *O wretched man that I am! who shall deliver me from the body of this death? I thank God through Jesus our Lord. So then with the mind I myself serve the law of God; but with the flesh the law of sin.* (Romans 7:24,25)

Finally, "I" finds that there is One who is sufficient. Struggling yields to power, defeat is changed to victory, misery is transformed into joy. When "I" goes out, Christ comes in.

The life "in Christ" is a wonderful thing. Paul says, *The law of the Spirit of life in Christ Jesus hath made me free from the law of sin and death.* This is what happens. When I step into an airplane, I am free from the law of gravity. The higher law that operates in the plane to lift it above the clouds, makes useless the law of gravity which but a few minutes before held me fast to the earth. The law of gravity is not destroyed but rendered inoperative. This is what happens in my life when I step "in Christ." The law that operates by the Spirit in my life lifts me above the world and sin, and sin no longer has dominion over me. I am free. I am without condemnation. Have you stepped into Christ? Are you living on a plane far above all principalities and powers?

Have you come to the end of "self"? Remember, "I" never brings anything but failure. It is the "I" in "s-I-n" that must be removed. Put "O" in its place and you have "SON." He will give you victory!

Step out of the self-life into the Spirit-filled life. In Romans 8 instead of the word "I," we find the word "Spirit" used twenty-one times. We must "yield" our lives to Him. This is our part. Then He will fill us with His Spirit. This is Christ's part.

This glorious chapter opens with "no condemnation," and ends with "no separation." This is a picture of our life "in Christ." The Christian is safe: Christ is around him; the Spirit is within him and God is for him.

> "Once I tried to use Him;
> Now He uses me."

HOW TO SERVE GOD (Read Romans 12–16)

I beseech you therefore, brethren, by the mercies of God, that ye present your bodies a living sacrifice, holy, acceptable unto God, which is your reasonable service. (Romans 12:1)

It may surprise you to find out that up to this point we have not had to do a thing but believe on Christ and yield ourselves to Him to use as He will. Now we are to serve! We are "saved to serve." We are Christ's representatives on this earth, to take His place; to spread His Gospel. Our life is the outworking of His glorious salvation.

Until we have been saved by His grace and transformed by His love, we can do little for God. Read I Corinthians 13. But when we present ourselves to Christ and become filled with His love we can find much to be done. Christ wants a "living sacrifice," not a dead one. (Romans 12:1) Many will die for Christ. Few will live for Him. There are many of you who would rather be burned at a stake than stand the ridicule of your associates. One definition of a modern Christian is "a person who will die for the church he will not attend." How many of us say nothing when Christ's name is brought into question or is used in vain!

Let others see Jesus in you! Live for Him, then you will be ready to die for Him.

The first half of Romans is what God did for us.

The last half of Romans is what we may do for God.

We find our Christian service in relation to

Minimum Daily Requirements / Spiritual Vitamins

Sunday: WHAT WE ARE BY NATURE Romans 1:14-23; 3:9-20

Monday: HOW TO BECOME A CHRISTIAN Romans 3:21–5:21

Tuesday: HOW TO LIVE A CHRISTIAN LIFE Romans 6:1-23

Wednesday: A STRUGGLE Romans 7:1-25

Thursday: THE LIFE OF VICTORY Romans 8:1-39

Friday: THE JEWS SET ASIDE Romans 9:30–11:12

Saturday: THE CHRISTIAN'S SERVICE Romans 12:1-21

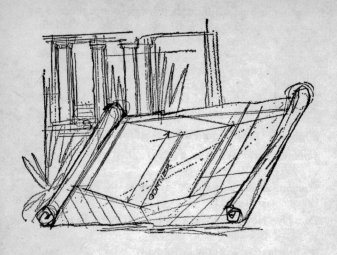

Chapter 8

LET'S LOOK AT I CORINTHIANS

*I CORINTHIANS PORTRAYS JESUS CHRIST,
OUR LORD*

Discover how many times the title, Lord Jesus Christ, is given in the first ten verses.

The name "Lord" is very prominent in this book. (I Cor. 1:31; 2:8,16; 3:20; 4:4; 5:4; 6:13, etc.) This is full of meaning, because all the trouble that had crept into the church at Corinth had come because they failed to recognize Jesus Christ as Lord. Crown Christ Lord of your life. He will bring order out of disorder.

The archeologist's spade is making Corinth live again! Corinth was the most important city of all Greece in Paul's day. Its wealth was fabulous. Men spent their days in tournaments and speeches. Luxury, dissipation and public immorality were rampant among this great industrial and seafaring population. Corinth attracted great crowds of foreigners from the East and West. Their gods were gods of pleasure and lust. There was, besides, much culture and art. The city abounded in studios of language and schools of philosophy. The boast of the day was that no one could walk along the streets without meeting a wise man.

As in most cities, there was a large colony of Jews who had kept a strong moral standard and held to their religious beliefs. But the city itself was the center of a debased form of the worship of Venus. The temple of this goddess was a monument of the vices of the city. Wandering preachers found an audience anywhere.

If we read Acts 18, we find how the Gospel reached this wicked city. The apostle Paul, then a man about fifty years of age, in the garb of a working man, entered the busy metropolis and went through its streets in search of a workshop where he might earn his own living. There were no billboards advertising the coming of a world-renowned evangelist. There were no headlines in the newspapers, reporting his meetings. Rather, this tradesman came into town and began his tentmaking. This was a leading industry in that day, like building is today. He went into business with the well-to-do tentmakers, Aquila and Priscilla. He was always able to support himself, making enough to carry on his missionary work. A wonderful work was done in Corinth during the year and a half that Paul was there. He began by speaking in the synagogues to mixed congregations of Jews and Greeks. He found hatred among the Jews and scorn among the Greeks.

I Corinthians is a difficult book to outline, but it takes up many wonderful subjects. It deals with Christian conduct. It is important how a Christian acts. Paul wrote his first letter to Corinth, to correct them about certain matters which had been reported to him as having crept into this church.

CORRECTIONS IN CHRISTIAN CONDUCT
(Read I Corinthians 1–11)

The wonderful church at Corinth, the brilliant jewel in the crown of Paul's labor, was failing. It all was because the worldliness (carnality) of the city had gotten within its walls. It was all right for the church to be in Corinth, but it was fatal when Corinth got into the church. It is a glorious sight to see a ship launched into the sea, but it is a tragic sight when the sea gets into the ship. The church of Christ should be set as a light in a dark place, but woe unto the church when the wickedness of the world invades it.

Practices common to this wicked city soon crept into the church. There were divisions among them; Christians going to law with Christians before heathen judges; behavior at the communion table was disgraceful; the women of the church no longer observed standards of modesty; the church membership was arguing over marriage and even spiritual gifts. Finally the church wrote Paul about these things, and asked his advice on the matter. These two books of Corinthians were written in answer to their requests.

The greatest danger of the Corinthian church was from within. This is always true. It is true of a nation. We must search for Satan lurking within the walls. He is Public Enemy No. 1.

Party Spirit

Paul speaks first of the divisions and cliques about which he had learned from friends and travelers. Nothing eats out the heart and life of the church like party politics. Christianity is LOVE. We have to be careful as Christians, because envy and strife in a church often go under the mask of zeal.

The Greek spirit of party politics had entered into the church, dividing it into parties, each trying to get the mastery. Their names are given in I Cor. 1:12. Paul, Apollos and Peter (Cephas) were parties named for their favorite teachers, and the Christ Party who held to that Name as if it did not belong to everyone in the church.

This dissension about religious leaders meant that the Christians at Corinth had slipped off center. There is only one Leader in every church. That Leader and center is Christ. If the church gets off center here, it goes off all down the line. A great fly-wheel on center moves quietly; off center it shakes the building to pieces. Christianity must be Christ-centered. If it is Christ-centered it is powerful. Christ Himself is the "good news." He did not only bring God's message; He was God's message. Paul, Peter, Apollos were all good men, but not God-men. How many are following religious leaders today rather than Christ Himself!

Jesus Christ is the only cure for division. (I Cor. 1:13) Every eye, every heart, every spirit must be turned to one object—Jesus Christ, our personal Saviour. Paul said, in effect, "Your party spirit is a sin. Can you follow a mere man, hoping that he can give you life? Was that man crucified for you? Trusting in what man has to say is foolish. Men see nothing in the cross of Christ. Christ alone has all the power and wisdom of God."

Youth and old age follow Christ to the cross and then stumble at the "blood" of the sacrifice. This is what the Jews and Greeks of Paul's day did. Shall we remove the cross from the Gospel because people do not like it? If we do, we remove the world's only way of salvation. We must preach "Christ crucified." It is not the teachings of Jesus that save men. His death alone can do that. The cross is the actual point at which God meets man.

81

THE CROSS

Unto the Jews a stumbling block—something they could not get over. (I Cor. 1:23) They could not understand how such a display of weakness as the cross could be a source of power. A man dying on a cross did not look much like a world Saviour to them. The scribes and Pharisees turned from the cross, and hatred filled their hearts. It meant failure to them. The Jews needed signs of power. They demanded something they could see and grasp. The Messiah must be a world Prince, a miracle worker. A multitude of Christians are like this today. They worship success as much as did the Jews. They despise weakness, and admire force. These people tell us that men of science are apt to stumble at the cross because they cannot explain how the blood of one Man could wash away the stain of sin.

Unto the Greeks foolishness. The Greeks regarded with contempt the unscientific religion first taught in an unschooled corner of the world like Nazareth, by the son of a carpenter who never studied at Athens or Rome. The Greeks idolized "brains." But God has never despised the humble things. He used David's slingshot to overcome Israel's worst enemy, the giant Goliath. He used the little boy's lunch to feed the multitude.

Either the cross is the "power of God" or it is "foolishness." If "foolishness," then you think it is unfit to do any good in your life. But listen! That condemns you, not the cross. If a boy is gazing at the sun at high noon, and says, "It is not bright," your answer could only be, "Friend, you had better see an oculist." You would know he was going blind. And if the cross seems "foolishness" to us, it is because we are already perishing, and our ability to understand the wisdom of God has gone.

No man ever leaves the cross in exactly the same condition as he came to it. He must receive it or reject it. If he receives it he becomes a son of God (John 1:12).

Paul did not preach Christ the conqueror, or Christ the philosopher, but Christ crucified, Christ the humble. Read his words in I Cor. 2:2. We live in a world which is like a puzzle. We do not need to know the plan of the whole maze, but we need merely to pass a line through our hands which will guide us to the secret of life. Christ crucified is that thread. He leads us to God.

Christianity is Christ—not creeds.

The fragile filament of an electric light will break at a touch, but will cooperate with the tremendous energy of electricity and produce a dazzling light. So we may be weak, frail, thin filaments, but in league with the Almighty God we become radiant lights to show forth His glory! This is what God wants of His ministers. Carey the cobbler, without God, was just a filament. With God, he became a great missionary light in India. Moody, without God, was just a pebble of humanity. With God, he became a rock of strength.

Paul says, *I judge not mine own self.* (I Cor. 4:3) Beware when you stand at the bar of your own conscience. When your conscience says to you, "You may do it," it is always well to go to Jesus Christ and say, "May I?" It is hard to be fair with ourselves. No man, no matter how honest he is, is permitted to judge his own cause.

Do not depend on man's judgment. The world judges our character upon a single act. Beware of your friend's judgment because he may be too favorable in his opinion of you. We like to believe all the good things said about us and resent any unfavorable criticism.

Paul says there is one judgment to which he will submit—one that is always right. *He that judgeth me is the Lord.* (I Cor. 4:4) I am Christ's steward and to

Him I am ultimately responsible. From His judgment there is no escape. His calm eyes are upon me.

A young violinist stood before a vast audience who was applauding his rendition with thunderous praise. He seemed to be deaf to it all. His eyes were on one who sat in the midst of the crowd. This was his teacher, one who was a past master in the art in which he was a beginner. Every change in his master's face meant more to him than the plaudits of the crowd. Not until the great master's head nodded approval did he accept his great ovation.

Little will it count for a man standing before the great white throne to say, "I held a very high place in the estimation of my neighbors. The newspapers blew my trumpet lustily. My name was carved on a marble statue which my fellow-citizens set up in my honor."

Seek praise from Him which is praise indeed. If He says, "Well done, good and faithful servant," what else matters!

VICE IN THE CHURCH

We, as Christians, must act out in our lives what we believe in our hearts. It is a serious thing to profess to live the life of a Christian. If we lower the standard Christ has set, we give the wrong testimony to the world. You are an epistle open and read of all men. What kind of a Gospel is "The Gospel According to You"?

An old story is told of a man who wished to hire a coachman to drive his six-horse carriage to his home over a mountainous road. He called in several men. To the first one he said, "How near to the edge of a cliff can you drive without going over?" "Oh, I think I could go within a foot and not go over." He called the next one and asked him the same question. "Oh, I am an expert. I can drive to the very edge and not go over."

Then he called the third. When he questioned this man, he answered, "Oh, if you want me to drive near the edge, I can't. I'd stay as far from it as I could." "You're the man I want. I'll take you."

Young people, don't let your life be so near the edge of questionable things that some day you will slide off. If you fall, others will fall with you. Watch your testimony.

Righteousness comes from God, but it must be shown in our daily walk. The Corinthians, living in the Hollywood of their day, needed admonition just as we do. Righteousness is from Christ, and for Christ. "What would Jesus do?" should be the test in every questionable thing of life. Christ in you is the secret and the way of life. This is the guiding principle for every life.

Dr. Ironside spoke to some Hopi Indians about the responsibility of living for Christ. At the conclusion, an Indian said, "Man with the iron voice, you have made the way very hard today. I thought when I was saved by grace, that was all, but now it looks as though I have to walk to heaven on the edge of a razor." God has saved us by His grace, but He has called us into a holy walk with Him.

KNOW YE?

This is one of Paul's expressions. His faith was built on facts. He wanted to know things. Underline the "know ye's" in chapter 6. What are we supposed to know?

Christ has paid a great price to purchase us, and it is His purpose to make us like Himself.

What? know ye not that your body is the temple of the Holy Ghost which is in you, which ye have of God, and ye are not your own? For ye are bought with a price: therefore glorify God in your body, and in your spirit, which are God's. (I Cor. 6:19,20)

If our bodies have been redeemed by the Lord Jesus Christ, then they no longer belong to us but to the One who purchased us with His precious blood. *Ye are bought with a price.*

A lad was sailing the little boat he had spent weeks in making. Suddenly a gust of wind snapped the string that held the small craft. It floated out and he could not reach it. His young heart was heavy. The thing which he had made was snatched from him. One day, some weeks later, he spied his boat in the window of a shop, with the price of $1.00 marked upon it. He went in to claim it as his own, but the shopman refused to give it to him, saying he would have to pay the price. The lad ran home and emptied his bank, and after he had paid the price the shopman demanded, he took the boat in his arms and said, "Little boat, you are twice mine. I made you and I bought you." This is exactly what our Lord Jesus Christ did. He created us, then He bought us. We are twice His! Yonder at Calvary was the market-place where the Saviour bought us with His blood, but "He never got His money's worth," an old Puritan writer said.

God used to have a temple for His people; now He has a people for a temple. When a man steps into the church, off comes his hat, for he realizes he has stepped into the sanctuary. But has he forgotten that the real sanctuary in which Christ dwells is his body? We are taught as boys and girls not to be noisy or boisterous in the church, for it is the house in which we meet God. How much more important that we remember that our body is His dwelling place and that we should do nothing to grieve Him.

LIBERTY NOT RECKLESSNESS

The Scripture does not lay down little rules for our conduct and tell us just the things we ought to do or not do, but rather states principles which should guide the Christian's actions. Someone has well said that Christian liberty does not mean the right to do as we like, but rather the right to do as we ought. Paul puts it, *All things are lawful unto me, but all things are not expedient.* (I Cor. 6:12)

A man was walking down the street swinging his arms out from his chest and by mistake, struck a passer-by in the face. The man struck was furious and started to strike back. "Hey, isn't this a free country? Can't a fellow do his exercises on the street if he wishes?" "Yes," was the answer, "but remember where my nose begins, your liberty ends."

Let this be in your mind constantly as far as your conduct is concerned. If your liberty harms another, then your liberty has gone too far.

Yes, I can do anything I want to, but I must be sure my desires are to please Christ. What I do is an example to others, and may harm or bless them. I should not only answer the question, "Does my action harm weaker Christians?" but "Does it glorify God?"

MARRIAGE

God states the principles of marriage very plainly. When people are married they take each other for life. Read what Jesus said, on divorce. Matthew 5:31,32; 19:3-11; Mark 10:2-12. These are plain words.

Mark I Cor. 7:9,13 in your Bible. Think over these verses. They will tell us much of our Christian responsibility to those who are not Christians.

THE LORD'S SUPPER

Paul gives a careful account of the beginning of the Lord's Supper and then tells of its value.

Established on the night of betrayal.

Celebrated in remembrance of Him.

Symbol of His body broken.

A new covenant in His blood.

A pledge of His coming again.

Not to eat or drink unworthily.

As oft as ye drink it, in remembrance of me. (See 11:25.) Christ wants us to remember Him! Think on Christ when you go to His table. He longs for your love!

INSTRUCTIONS IN CHRISTIAN CONDUCT
(Read I Corinthians 12–16)

In I Corinthians 12, we see the gifts that the Spirit gives to believers. In verses 1-3, he tells of the change that had come into the lives of these Corinthian Christians when they turned from worshiping dead idols to the living Christ. In order that they might develop in their Christian life, Christ gave them the gifts of the Spirit. (I Cor. 12:4-11) One cannot teach the Scriptures unless the Spirit gives him wisdom. One must pray "in the Spirit" and to sing acceptably to God it must be "in the Spirit." Sometimes we say when we look at a successful Christian, "My, he is a man of natural abilities," when really he has received many gifts from the Spirit.

When the Holy Spirit guides the life of the church, there will be harmony. It is like the boats of Ancient Greece. The oarsmen were separated from one another by partitions over which they could not see. As many as 200 men were used to man these great three-decked vessels, and no one could see his fellow oarsmen. But their strokes were in perfect time and in such harmony that in time of battle they often drove the nose of the vessel into an approaching enemy ship with such speed as to send it crashing through its timbers, cutting it in two and driving it to the bottom of the sea. How was this perfect unity accomplished? By the director who stood at the rear of the vessel, baton in hand, and every oarsman answered to the time as he beat it. Being in unison with the director, every stroke came together and this cooperation made them invincible. This is what Christ wants in His Church. He wants all of us under the direction of the Spirit driving ahead against the enemy and winning victories over sin.

GOD'S LOVE CHAPTER

The way to use these gifts that the Spirit gives is beautifully told in I Corinthians 13. This chapter is called the Hymn of Love. Gifts without love are but poor things. People talk of love but they do not live the way they speak. Until the love of Christ is in a heart it is impossible for men to love one another really. Men seem to worship force. But history shows us that the victories of force do not last. Napoleon discovered this. He said, "Alexander the Great, Julius Caesar, Charlemagne and myself all founded kingdoms upon force, but they have all crumbled to dust. Jesus Christ founded His Kingdom upon love, and today millions would die for Him."

THE PILLARS OF PAUL'S GOSPEL

No doubt there was a group in the Corinthian church who did not believe in the resurrection of the dead. Paul in answering this starts out by giving a wonderful statement of what the Gospel is in I Cor. 15:1-11. Paul did not give a new Gospel. It was the old Gospel, given in Genesis, Exodus, Leviticus.

1. Christ died for our sins according to the Scriptures. (15:3)
2. He was buried. (15:4)

3. He rose again the third day according to the Scriptures. (15:4)

4. He was seen of many witnesses. (15:5,6)

If we deny the resurrection, we deny one of the greatest of all truths of the Gospel. But more than all that, no resurrection would mean no Gospel at all, for we would be worshiping a dead Christ. There would be no "good news," for there would be no proof that God had accepted Christ's death as an atonement for our sins. If a sailor on jumping overboard to rescue a drowning man were drowned himself, then we would know that he did not save the man after whom he went. If Christ did not come out from the grave, then He could not bring anyone with Him from the grave. Christ's body died and it was His body that was raised again. His soul was committed into the hands of the Father.

Because Christ lives, we shall live also. *O death, where is thy sting? O grave, where is thy victory?*

Minimum Daily Requirements / Spiritual Vitamins
Sunday: DIVISIONS IN THE CHURCH I Cor. 1:10-31
Monday: HUMAN WISDOM I Cor. 2:1-16
Tuesday: WORLDLINESS IN THE CHURCH I Cor. 3:1-23
Wednesday: IMMORALITY IN THE CHURCH I Cor. 5:1-13
Thursday: THE LORD'S SUPPER I Cor. 11:1-34
Friday: HYMN OF LOVE I Cor. 13:1-13
Saturday: THE RESURRECTION I Cor. 15:1-58

Chapter 9

LET'S LOOK AT II CORINTHIANS

II CORINTHIANS PORTRAYS JESUS CHRIST,
OUR SUFFICIENCY

Paul was somewhat worried as to how the church at Corinth would receive his first letter. He wondered how they had accepted his rebukes, so he sent Titus, and perhaps Timothy, to Corinth to find out the effect of his epistle. During Paul's third missionary journey, while he was in Philippi, Titus reported that the majority of the church had received the letter in the proper spirit. But there were those who doubted his motives, and even denied his apostleship, saying that he did not have the proper credentials for an apostle. Perhaps they questioned this because he was not one of

91

the original Twelve. These enemies were bitter and tried to undermine him and his authority.

Under these circumstances he wrote his second epistle, to express his joy over the encouraging news of how his first epistle had been received, and to defend his apostleship.

Paul gives more of his personal history in this letter than in any of his other epistles. He reveals his courage and his self-sacrificing love. He speaks of glorying or boasting thirty-one times, because he was compelled to. Read II Corinthians 12:11. *I am become a fool in glorying; ye have compelled me: for I ought to have been commended of you: for in nothing am I behind the very chiefest apostles, though I be nothing.*

Paul tells us of some things which happened in his life, that are revealed only in this letter.

His escape from Damascus in a basket. (11:32,33)

His experience of being caught up to the third heaven. (12:1-4)

His thorn in the flesh. (12:7)

His unusual suffering. (11:23-27)

He told none of these until he was compelled to, to prove that if he wanted to boast, he had good reason to do so.

PAUL'S MINISTRY (Read II Corinthians 1–7)

Paul opens this second epistle with his usual greeting and thanksgiving. (II Cor. 1:1-3) Everyone loves a true story. Paul tells so many personal experiences of his life in this letter that it makes everyone love to read it. He begins by telling of the great trouble through which he has been passing. Through all of his trials he had learned to know God better. God is always made more real to us in times of sorrow. We find that God never fails.

Paul's sufferings in Asia were of a very serious nature. Very likely he went through a dangerous sickness in which they despaired of his life. (II Cor. 1:4-11) He appreciated their prayers and now he was appealing to their love and sympathy. He wanted them to be ready for much that he was to write about, concerning the defense of his apostleship.

Paul had a clear conscience as to his sincerity and faithfulness while he labored among them. He explained that he sent his first letter instead of coming himself, that when he did come he might be able to praise and not scold them. (II Cor. 1:23–2:4) To this statement he calls God to witness.

The Judaizing teachers (or law teachers) of Paul's day always carried letters of introduction with them. They were Paul's chief trouble-makers. They tried in every way to fight him. We hear them asking, "Who is this Paul? What letters of recommendation from Jerusalem does he have?" How foolish this question was to Paul! Did he need a letter of recommendation to a church which he himself had established? *Why,* he answers, *ye are our epistle written in our hearts, known and read of all men.* (II Cor. 3:2) This letter is not written with ink upon paper, but with the Spirit on Christian hearts.

The lives of true Christians at Corinth served as letters to recommend both Paul the servant and Christ the Lord. Men read men. Living epistles are read when Bible epistles are not. Remember your life is an open letter. Christian lives are about the only religious books the world reads. They do not study God's Word but they do study church members. This gives us a great opportunity for good, for we may lead men to Christ. It also carries a great possibility of evil, for we may drive men from Christ. If ever Christian living were necessary it is now.

Paul's ministry is a triumphant one, but it is filled with suffering. Warfare always is full of illustrations of triumph through suffering. Victory costs! Paul tells us much about his tribulations. (II Cor. 4; 6; 11) When he was so gloriously converted, the Lord said, *I will show him how great things he must suffer for my name's sake*. (Acts 9:16) It seems as though the trials began immediately, and followed his pathway for thirty years. But Paul was always optimistic because he knew that afflictions here would increase glory beyond. (II Cor. 4:17,18)

The pessimist sees a difficulty in every opportunity.

The optimist sees an opportunity in every difficulty.

Paul could sing as he suffered, for he knew the wonderful grace of God. He was always conscious of the presence of the Lord Jesus Christ. He knew that the greater the suffering in this present world, the greater the glory of eternity. (II Cor. 4:8-18) Paul lived with his eye on the future! He was a dealer in futures!

Christ nowhere promises that a Christian will be free from suffering or sorrow. Rather do we hear that *in the world ye shall have tribulation*. (John 16:33) Christ allows us to get into trouble that He may deliver us. He allowed Daniel to be put into the den of lions that He might pull him out. He allowed Shadrach, Meshach, and Abednego to go into the fiery furnace that He might deliver them. He allowed Paul to be shipwrecked that He might save him. Our God is able to deliver!

Paul finds his comfort through all his troubles in the fact of the resurrection. He lived under the inspiration of the fact that one day he was to have a changed, glorified body. Our suffering bodies will soon be exchanged for painless glorified bodies. Whether we live or die, we must keep this reward in view. *For we must all appear before the judgment seat of Christ; that every one may receive the things done in his body, according to that he hath done, whether it be good or bad.* **(II Cor. 5:10)**

The aim of Paul's ministry is that men may be reconciled to God. (II Cor. 5:20) Men are God's greatest concern. As Christ's ambassador he makes his appeal to men of the world.

He follows this with an appeal to holy living (6:11–7:16). Holy living means wholly unto God. Read these verses, everyone! He appeals to his fellow-workers not to receive God's loving-kindness in vain, but to open their hearts to Him. God demands a clean and separated life. He wants Christians to separate themselves from unbelievers. They were living in a heathen atmosphere and the Corinthians were lax in their morals.

LIBERAL GIVING (Read II Corinthians 8; 9)

Paul tells the church at Corinth of the generosity of the churches of Macedonia to the Palestine Famine Fund. Although poor themselves, they begged for an opportunity to give, and they gave liberally because first they gave themselves to the Lord. The fund was gathered from all the churches of Asia Minor and Greece. It had been started a year before. (8:10) Paul was in Macedonia at the time he wrote this. He had accepted no pay for his work from any of the churches except Philippi. Christ was the example of these early Christians. (II Cor. 8:9)

HOW TO GIVE

Give out of your poverty......................(8:2)
Give generously ....(8:3)
Give willingly ....(9:7)
Give proportionately ....(8:12,13,14)
Give cheerfully ....(9:7)
Give bountifully ....(9:6)

All this was because they first gave themselves to Christ. The Lord knows that if He gets us, He will get our gifts and our service.

A young soldier called his mother from New York. She hadn't heard his voice for twenty months. "Hello, Mom; this is Tom. I'm coming home. What can I bring you? I want to bring you something because I love you heaps, Mom." From the other end of the wire a voice, broken with emotion and joy, said tenderly, "Nothing, dear. I don't want anything but just you. Come home as fast as you can. I just can't wait to see you." This is what Jesus wants. He knows that if He has us, He will get our love and our service.

God has ever promised to reward the generous giver. (9:6) He enriches us with spiritual graces as well as with material things. These gifts strengthened the ties of brotherhood between the Jewish and Gentile Christians. *Thanks be unto God for His unspeakable Gift!* (II Cor. 9:15)

This is the reason for our giving, *for God so loved the world, that He gave His only begotten Son*. God himself delights to give.

Someone asked Captain Levy of Philadelphia how he was able to give so much and still have so much left. "Oh," said he, "as I shovel out, He shovels in; and the Lord has a bigger shovel than I have."

PAUL'S APOSTLESHIP (Read II Corinthians 10–13)

The charge against Paul by some in the church was that he was a coward. He was bold in his writings, but was weak in personality. The New Testament gives us no suggestion as to what Paul looked like. To imagine that this man, who turned city after city upside down, was weak is absurd. He was a powerful and dominating person. He was a man of outstanding gifts and had a keen and inquiring mind. Beside this, Christ lived in him and worked through him. He was hidden behind the cross.

His enemies said that no apostle would work with his own hands and support himself. They pointed to the other apostles, but Paul explained that he had the right to receive pay, yet refused it lest his example be abused by those false teachers who would commercialize the ministry. He declared that at least he founded his own churches and did not go around troubling churches founded by others, as they were doing.

WRONG STANDARDS OF MEASURE

They measuring themselves by themselves, and comparing themselves among them, are not wise. (II Cor. 10:12-18)

We all have a tendency to take a wrong standard for measuring character. We compare ourselves among ourselves. We conclude we are "as good as the average." But average Christians are not what the Bible requires. Let us pray Wesley's prayer, "Lord make me an extraordinary Christian." Like the businessman who compares his weights and measures with the great government standards, we have a true test when we compare ourselves with the standard of Christ. When a man five feet six inches tall compares himself with a man five feet three inches tall, he concludes he is of quite good size. But how he shrinks when you place him beside a man six feet two! Are you comparing yourselves with average Christians or with Christ in your character, self-sacrifice and consecration?

Paul in Third Heaven

He was caught up into "Paradise," even to the third heaven. You recall that Jesus went into Paradise at His death. (Luke 23:43) There Paul had been given marvelous visions and revelations, and heard things that could not be put into speech. (12:4) No doubt no human language could describe the glory. It would have been like trying to picture a sunset to a man born blind. Paul had nothing to compare it with that we could understand.

It seemed as though because of these heavenly experiences God allowed Paul to suffer a physical weakness. The Lord knows the danger of pride of heart after such an experience, and so He permitted "a messenger of Satan to buffet him." He himself called his affliction "a thorn in the flesh." (12:7) There have been many speculations as to what this "thorn" really was. It would appear that God had left out just what it was that all might know that the grace which was sufficient for Paul in his trouble would be enough for any thorn given to man.

WHY THORNS?

Many wonder why God does not remove "thorns" from the flesh when we pray to Him. We must learn that God always answers prayer, but sometimes the answer is "No." He knows it will be better for us to bear the thorn than be without it. "Thorns" in the flesh have made many a man lean on Christ.

Dr. Moon, the brilliant man whose blind eyes made him give to the world the system of reading that others with blind eyes might know the joy of acquiring knowledge, came to the realization that his "thorn" was a blessing. Sometimes a "thorn" is a warning to keep us from sin and failure. God proved to Paul that no matter what his weakness was, His strength was sufficient.

Someone said to a humble Christian woman, rich toward God: "Are you the woman with the great faith?" "Oh, no," said she; "I am the woman with a little faith in a great God!"

A minister one day buried his only child. He went into his study the next day to prepare his message for Sunday, but he could not. His grief was too great. Through his tears, which would insist upon coursing down his cheeks, his eyes fell on these words: "My grace is sufficient." It seemed to read this way: "My grace IS sufficient." He wrote it that way on a card and hung it in front of his desk. He learned to know a God who is always present. Every word is important. Examine it word for word.

My—means God.

Grace—unmerited favor. I bring Christ what I have, my sin. He brings me what He has—His righteousness. The exchange is made. He takes my sin and gives me His righteousness. This is grace, wonderful grace!

Is—the present, always.

Sufficient—enough and to spare. *Our sufficiency is of God.* (3:5) Here is where Spurgeon laughed out loud. "To think," said he, "that our little cups could exhaust the ocean of His grace."

We are satisfied with Jesus. Is He your personal comfort? God gives us unusual strength for unusual tasks. Paul says, *When I am weak, then am I strong.* (12:10)

It is when we are going through the sorrows of life that we discover our real friends. Suffering and trouble have done more than anything else to let men know what a great God they have. What a great God Daniel knew he had, when he was in the lions' den! What a great God the three young men in the fiery furnace knew as their champion!

There is strength and courage in the heart in which Christ is dwelling.

II Corinthians closes with the benediction which today brings to a close many a church service. Here it is. *The grace of the Lord Jesus Christ, and the love of God, and the communion of the Holy Ghost, be with you all. Amen.* (II Cor. 13:14)

Minimum Daily Requirements / Spiritual Vitamins

Sunday: CHRIST OUR COMFORT II Cor. 1:1–2:17
Monday: LIVING EPISTLES II Cor. 3:1–4:18
Tuesday: AMBASSADORS FOR CHRIST II Cor. 5:1–6:18
Wednesday: THE HEART OF PAUL II Cor. 7:1–8:15
Thursday: CHRISTIAN GIVING II Cor. 8:16–9:15
Friday: PAUL'S APOSTLESHIP II Cor. 10:1–11:33
Saturday: GOD'S STRENGTH II Cor. 12:1–13:14

Chapter 10

LET'S LOOK AT GALATIANS

GALATIANS PORTRAYS JESUS CHRIST,
OUR LIBERTY

This epistle has done more than any other book in the New Testament to free our Christian faith from Judaism (law), Roman Catholicism, and ritualism which has threatened the simple Gospel of the Lord Jesus Christ. So many people want to do something to be saved. The question of the Philippian jailor, *What must I do to be saved?* is the question multitudes ask. The answer is always the same. *Believe on the Lord Jesus Christ, and thou shalt be saved.* (Acts 16:31)

A religion without the cross is not Christ's religion. Christ did not come merely to blaze a trail through a tangled forest, or to set us an example of true living. He came to be a Saviour. A gospel without the print of the nails is not the Gospel of Christ.

This epistle of Galatians is the Christian's Declaration of Independence. Our battle hymn is "Christus Liberator." *If the Son therefore shall make you free, ye shall be free indeed.* Many imagine that restrictions destroy liberty. The opposite is true. On entering a free public park, the first thing we see is, "Don't walk on the grass," "No dogs allowed," "Don't pick the flowers." And yet this is a free park! We do not complain. These laws preserve the park. Were they not enacted it would be no more a park than any vacant lot in the neighborhood. Thus it is with society at large. If we should revolt against God and His order, civilization would lapse into barbarism. This is what is happening in the world today. Liberty is not freedom from law— that is recklessness. Liberty is freedom in law. Paul speaks of the liberty we have *in Christ,* (Gal. 2:4) for *where the Spirit is Lord, there is liberty.* (II Cor. 3:17, Rotherham.) This is the one great secret of liberty.

INTRODUCTION (Read Galatians 1:1-11)

What was this Gospel Paul preached? Paul's Gospel shuts out all works. *Knowing that a man is not justified by the works of the law, but by the faith of Jesus Christ . . . for by the works of the law shall no flesh be justified.* (Gal. 2:16) The difficulty about salvation is not that we should be good enough to be saved but that we should see that we are bad enough to need salvation. Christ can only save sinners.

Paul shows us the seriousness of our condition outside Christ. When a medical specialist says, "Your only hope is this or that," you know what a critical and serious condition you must be in. Here are the words of a great Gospel expert. Paul declares that our position is so serious that the Gospel of the grace of God is our only hope.

102

PAUL DEFENDS HIS APOSTLESHIP
(Read Galatians 1:12–2:21)

Paul did not consult with anyone as to what he should preach, but retired to the wilds of Arabia for three years and listened to God. He was taught by the Spirit. He had only been with Peter and James fifteen days after the three years in Arabia, so he couldn't have learned much from them.

Paul ended his great apology by a personal word of testimony which gives us a complete picture of the Christian life both positively and negatively. *I am crucified with Christ: nevertheless I live; yet not I, but Christ liveth in me: and the life which I now live in the flesh I live by the faith of the Son of God, who loved me, and gave Himself for me.* (Gal. 2:20) It is a paradox indeed.

This verse is true of every believer. We do not need to be crucified with Christ. We have been crucified with Him. He died in my place. Now we live not by law but by faith. Christ was our Sacrifice for sin, our sufficiency for the new life.

PAUL DEFENDS THE GOSPEL
(Read Galatians 3:1–4:31)

"I've tried religion for the past five years and it hasn't worked. I gave it up," were the words of a young man when a preacher asked him to accept Christ. "Why, I tried religion for fifteen years and it did nothing for me. I gave it up, too," the preacher said. A pause followed. "Then why are you a minister?" the youth asked. "Then I tried Christ, and He fully met my needs. It is not religion I am recommending to you, but a living, loving Saviour."

People who do not believe in foreign missions say that the heathen have their own religion and why disturb them? Yes, they have so much religion that they are bowed down under the weight of the load, but no "good news" of the Gospel. It is the Gospel we are commanded to preach to every creature. A great bishop once said, "I wouldn't go across the street to give a pagan religion, but I would go around the world to offer him Christ."

Have you ever thought how strange the following statement is? What would you say if someone came up to you and said, "I've good news for you"? On inquiring what it is, he says, "So-and-so is dead!" You would be horrified. Yet the apostles went about after Christ's death declaring it as good news. This is the only death to be proclaimed as glad tidings, the death on Calvary. Of all the countless deaths upon the earth, only one could be called gospel. The gospel is God's spell. It was a story that cast a wonderful spell upon its hearers.

Religion is the best man can do. Christianity is the best God can do. See the results of man's best. *For by the works of the law shall no flesh be justified.* (Gal. 2:16) How can a man be made just? *By the faith of Jesus Christ.* (2:16) Christianity is God's best.

It is hard for us to believe that the priceless gift of forgiveness of sins and the gift of the Holy Spirit are not gained by real effort, but God offers them to us free of charge. Why not take them? Why worry about our own unworthiness? Why not accept them with thankfulness?

Immediately foolish reason says, "If people don't have to do a thing for their salvation or for an atonement for their wrongdoings, then they will become shiftless and will not even try to do good." But we have found that when we have accepted the Gospel with a thankful heart then we get busy on good works. We want to please God. Those who think we ought to be saved by our works think faith is an easy thing, but we know from personal experience how hard it is to simply believe. Luther tells us that a Christian is not sinless, but God no longer chalks sin against him because of his faith in Christ.

ABRAHAM'S EXAMPLE

Even as Abraham believed God, and it was accounted to him for righteousness. (Gal. 3:6) Abraham may have had a good standing with men for his upright life, but not with God. In God's sight, Abraham was a condemned sinner. You see righteousness had been given to Abraham on the ground of his faith, not his works. If faith without works was sufficient for Abraham, why should we turn from faith to law? *Abraham believed.* That is faith. Faith says to God, "I believe what you say."

The law cannot give righteousness but it does bring death upon all those who do not keep it. (3:10) Law demands perfect obedience. Many think that they should get something for keeping the law. Really they should get nothing. Men ought to keep the law and get nothing for doing so. You live in a city all your life and during your lifetime you keep the laws of that city. Will the city council present you with a gift because you have not broken the laws? Of course not. You ought to keep the law. But suppose after twenty years of law-keeping you then commit a crime. The authorities will then give you something—a jail sentence for breaking it. The Bible tells us that a curse (a sentence) is upon all who break the law, while a blessing is upon all those who live by faith.

THE LAW'S WORK

The law deals with what we are and do, while grace deals with what Christ is and does. What good is the law? We find the answer in Gal. 3:19,20. Everything has its purpose. The law is given to restrain the wicked by giving a punishment for crime, just as civil laws keep men from murder and theft because of the fear of jail or the electric chair. These restraints do not make men righteous but restrain them from crime.

Law reveals sin but does not remove it. The law proves that every man is a sinner by nature and directs him to Christ! We so often think that we become sinners when we commit some sinful acts. But it is because we are already sinners that we commit the act. A man lies because he is a liar. He steals because he is a thief. He does not become a liar when he utters the lie. It only proves he is a liar.

The law, too, was given to drive us to Christ by showing us our need. The Gospel tells us that Christ is the only One who can meet the need. (Gal. 3:23–4:11) Paul says that the law was our schoolmaster to shock us into a sense of our need of Christ that we might be justified by faith in Him. (3:24) God's law is not like the cruel schoolmaster of former times, a regular tyrant. His law is not to torment us always. God's law is like the good schoolmaster who trains his children to find pleasure in doing the things they formerly detested.

The law really has a place in leading us into a Christian experience. Did you ever see anyone trying to sew without a needle? That person would make poor speed if she sewed with only a thread. This is like God's dealing with us. He puts the needle of the law first, for we sleep so soundly in our own sins that we need to be aroused by something sharp. Then when He has the needle of the law fairly in our hearts, He draws a lifelong thread of Gospel love and peace.

Paul tells us that all are not the children of God. We find that it is faith in Christ, not works of the law, nor the Fatherhood of God, nor the brotherhood of man that makes us children of God. *For ye are all the children of God by faith in Christ Jesus.* (Gal. 3:26) It is faith, not works, that puts us into the family of God.

PAUL DESIRES THE GOSPEL BE APPLIED
(Read Galatians 5; 6)

The Gospel of Grace guards against recklessness. (5:13-15) *Ye have been called unto liberty; only use not liberty for an occasion to the flesh.* (Gal. 5:13)

Many people are afraid to live under grace instead of law for fear it will lead men to "live as they please and do as they like." Grace will always lead a man to live as God pleases and like what He likes.

See how the flesh "acts up." Read this list of its seventeen evil works, 5:19-21. These are sins of the mind as well as the body. This is what we are by nature and these are the things that we do. Christ has given the Holy Spirit to make us free from these. *Walk in the Spirit, and ye shall not fulfil the lust of the flesh.* Let the Holy Spirit rule your life.

A child begins to walk by someone holding on to his hand. We begin our walk by the Spirit holding on to us.

The fault of so many Christians is that after they are converted they do not cut loose from their old habits and worldly friends and unbelief. They are like the drunken man who went down to the wharf at night, got into his boat but forgot to untie it. He rowed till morning but when the sun arose he saw he was just where he had started because he had never loosed himself from the dock. That is what happens to many Christians who never grow. They never pull up anchor and the world has a strong hold on them. They work hard but never get anywhere.

In contrast to the work of the flesh we see the ninefold fruit of the Spirit. (5:22-23) If we abide in Christ (John 15), we shall be free to bear fruit for God. Are we showing this cluster of fruit in our lives?

NINE GRACES

Toward God	Toward Others	Toward Myself
Love	Longsuffering	Faith
Joy	Gentleness	Meekness
Peace	Goodness	Temperance

"The harvest will not be according to how much we know, but how much we sow." We may have a large supply of seed in the barn of the mind but unless it is planted it will bear no harvest.

So many deceive themselves by saying it doesn't matter what I sow if I am sincere. Would that be good advice for a farmer? Self-life will never produce the fruit of the Spirit. *Whatsoever a man soweth, that shall he also reap.* (6:7)

Paul bore in his body the *slave marks of Jesus.* I belong to another. The Greek word "stigmata" means a brand, a mark, sometimes burnt into the face, body or arm of a slave.

What were Paul's stigmata? They were scars he had received by persecution and hardship endured for Christ. (II Cor. 6:4; 11:23)

The false teachers had come armed with letters of authority. I am without letters of recommendation. But behold my scars! They constitute my commission.

In Christ we are free to know the boundless life that is in Him. In Him we are "a new creature." (Gal. 6:15) Paul cries, *God forbid that I should glory, save in the cross of our Lord Jesus Christ, by whom the world is crucified unto me, and I unto the world.* (Gal. 6:14) *Let the world go by! I have Christ, and having Him, I have all.*

Minimum Daily Requirements / Spiritual Vitamins

Sunday: Only One Gospel Galatians 1:1-24

Monday: Justified by Faith Galatians 2:1-21

Tuesday: The Law Points to Christ Galatians 3:1-29

Wednesday: Law and Grace Galatians 4:1-31

Thursday: Stand Fast in Christian Liberty
Galatians 5:1-16

Friday: Flesh Versus Spirit Galatians 5:17-26

Saturday: Sowing and Reaping Galatians 6:1-18

Chapter 11

LET'S LOOK AT EPHESIANS

EPHESIANS PORTRAYS JESUS CHRIST,
OUR ALL IN ALL

This book shows us the great mystery of the Church. The real Church is the Body of Christ, and believers are members of that sacred Body of which Christ is the head.

Imagine for a moment that the Body is like a great building. The "stones" are redeemed human beings. Christ occupies the great throne room, or "Head." All the parts are like "rooms" in the building. Come with Paul through this glorious structure.

We approach in these chapters, one after another, six magnificent rooms in this great temple. They are all "in Christ." Let the scenes of this book be laid in each of these rooms successively.

THE ANTE-ROOM (Read Ephesians 1)

Let us enter this sacred Temple with hushed voices and bared heads. Christ is going to allow us to go into His holy presence. The door opens into the spacious Ante-Room, where we read upon the walls our standing with God through Jesus Christ. *Blessed . . . with all spiritual blessings. Chosen . . . in Him before the foundation of the world. Holy and without blame before Him in love. Accepted in the beloved.* These are some great wall mottoes for Christians. It will tax every spiritual energy to live up to them. Tremblingly we take our shoes from off our feet for the place whereon we stand is holy ground!

The blessings the Lord gives to the Christian are not only "heavenly" but *in the heavenlies.* Go through this first chapter and mark all you find "in Christ."

Was this always our position? (Ephesians 2:11-13)

We learn on entering this Temple that our calling and position have been planned and worked out by God the Father, the Son, and the Holy Spirit before the foundation of the world. (1:4) Every Christian should know his calling above everything else. The true knowledge of it will govern his life.

When a fellow is put on a football team, he must learn first to what position he has been chosen. Then he must know the rules of the game. All this governs his actions and his moves. We are playing the game of life. Let us find our calling in Christ, then as Paul says in Ephesians 4:1, *Walk worthy of the vocation wherewith ye are called.*

OUR SALVATION

The Father planned it......................1:4-6
The Son paid for it......................1:7-12
The Spirit applied it..................1:13,14
In whom we have redemption through His blood, the

forgiveness of sins, according to the riches of His grace.
(Eph. 1:7)

Redemption is the most glorious work of God. It is greater far than His work of creation. He spoke a word and worlds were formed, but it cost Him the life of His beloved Son to redeem the world. Paul delighted to dwell on this theme.

A king once offered a subject a very magnificent present for some service. "This is too much for me to receive," the man said. "But it is not too much for me to give," was the king's reply. He was rich and gave according to his ability to give. God is very rich and very loving and when He gives it is "according to the riches of His grace." Let us receive and estimate at its true worth God's gift of redemption. *Thanks be unto God for His unspeakable gift.* (II Cor. 9:15)

THE AUDIENCE CHAMBER OF THE KING
(Read Ephesians 2)

Next we are conducted into the glorious Audience Chamber of the King, into the Divine Presence. We have *access by one Spirit unto the Father.* (2:18) We would tremble as we entered if we did not hear the gracious words sound out, *You hath He quickened, who were dead in trespasses and sins: . . . . hath raised us up together, and made us sit together in heavenly places in Christ Jesus.* (2:1,6) But best of all, there is a sweet Voice sounding through the corridors, Welcome here! *Now therefore ye are no more strangers and foreigners, but fellow-citizens with the saints, and of the household of God.* (2:19) All of this is in sharpest contrast to what we were "in time past." (2:11-13) We once were "far off." Now we are "nigh." Humbly and thankfully we bow in glad acceptance of His love.

In this Audience Chamber, we find that God has made both Jew and Gentile "one" in Christ. We can better understand this by an illustration told by Dr.

Keller of Hunan Bible Institute in China. A barber, an occupation held in contempt in China, was marvelously converted. He had been an opium addict and a moral degenerate. In desperation he had come to the missionaries and prayer was answered for him. His appetite for opium left and he became a living witness for Christ.

During the barber's stay in the mission, a young man of the "student class" came as an inquirer but seeing the barber he refused to go in. One day thinking the barber had gone, he entered the mission and met the barber. Being too polite not to speak to him, he engaged in conversation. The barber told of the wonderful change that had come into his life through Christ. Class barriers melted away. The barber soon was a guest in the student's home, surrounded with wealth and culture. Christ had "made both one." This is what Christ will do with Jew and Gentile, slave and free man. Christ makes each one a new man and gives access into the very Audience Chamber of the King.

God is producing a Masterpiece, His Church. He says, *For we are His workmanship.* (2:10) This comes from the Greek word "poiema"—poem or masterpiece.

In Ephesians 1, we find how God planned and worked in the production of this Masterpiece. We were *chosen in Christ* to be holy and blameless. (1:4) In the ages of past eternity God was thinking about us, loving us, and planning to bless us. Know this, before Satan ever appeared to spoil the happiness of the man upon this earth, God made plans to make all who would believe on Him to be blameless.

"But God"—see God act! He changes all by His touch! This "But God" is the bridge which leads men out of their dark and hopeless condition. (2:4) When all human strength is at an end—"But God." Remember Christ comes to give life to the dead.

A quaint old legend tells of a piece of marble crying

from a pile of material which had been left as rubbish after a great building had been erected. It was saying, "Glory, glory!" A passer-by hearing the cry, stopped. He learned from the marble half-covered with dust and rubbish that Michelangelo had just passed by and said, "I see an angel in that stone." Now he had gone to get his mallet and chisel.

Humanity was like that stone in the heap, broken and useless, but the great Sculptor saw it and began His Masterpiece. As Michelangelo saw the angel in the old stone, so God sees the image of His Son in wretched humanity. The grace of God carved a Mueller out of the family scapegrace, a John B. Gough out of a barroom wreck.

The greatest proof of Christianity is that it has produced a New Man who is approved unto God. Only God could make a Paul out of Saul, and out of sinners make a new creation.

Salvation is the gift of God. *For by grace are ye saved through faith; and that not of yourselves: it is the gift of God.* (2:8) Faith is a gift, too. *Faith cometh by hearing.* (Rom. 10:17) Faith is the channel of salvation. It is the hand that receives the gift. It connects man with God.

THE THRONE ROOM (Read Ephesians 3)

Standing at the doors of the Throne Room are the stalwart guards of Law. They demand: "Who goes there? Why do you come? What are your credentials?" I answer feebly, "A sinner; I come to see the Lamb. I have nothing to recommend me for admittance." Then I hear the Voice of the Lamb from within, the call of the Son of Grace. "It is one of my sheep. Invite him in. My blood covers all. He needs no credentials." And Grace brings me past the stern guards of Law unto the throne of His mercy.

We have boldness and access with confidence by the faith of Him. (3:12) What a piling up of words to persuade us of our privilege and position as Christian believers! We are "accepted in the Beloved."

Here we behold the King! With Paul, we bow our knee *unto the Father of our Lord Jesus Christ, of whom the whole family in heaven and earth is named.* (3:14,15) Is posture a small thing? Kneeling is the attitude of humility, confession and entreaty. Remember the holiest of all men have approached God this way. David, Solomon, and Daniel knelt upon their knees. These men stooped to conquer; knelt to prevail.

When in Denmark we went up to one of the churches to look at Thorvaldsen's beautiful figure of the Christus. As we approached an old guard said, "If you wish to see His face, you must kneel." How true this is!

The word "mystery" which occurs three times here does not mean something mysterious. It merely means it is hidden until the appropriate time comes for God to reveal it. *Which in other ages was not made known . . . as it is now revealed,* Paul says.

The mystery of the Church is that the Gentiles are to have an equal position with the Jews, God's chosen people. (Ephesians 3:6) All this was "by faith." (Rom. 15:9, 10; Gal. 3:8, 9)

Let us lift our voices in this Throne Room in hosannas to our King. (Eph. 3:20, 21)

ABLE—ABUNDANTLY—ABOVE—ALL—GOD

He is able to do all that we ask or think.

He is able to do above all that we ask or think.

He is able to do abundantly above all that we ask or think.

He is able to do exceeding abundantly above all that we ask or think.

115

If we are to enjoy this life in the Temple of God, we must be yielded in obedience to Him. If we yield to His plan for our lives as willing subjects, we will find that in His hand our lives will be filled with joy and beauty.

The great Paganini, world-famed violinist, was playing before a vast audience, when in the midst of a brilliant performance one of the strings of his violin snapped. He played on as if nothing had happened, but a second failed him. With two strings he proceeded to finish, when alas, a third string broke. But this master went on without faltering. He went to the end with such skill that his audience burst into a thunderous applause. Paganini was but a man, but our Master Musician is God. We may feel as if we were not gifted, a person with but one string. But if we place the instrument of our lives in His hand, He will bring forth real music by the skill of His hand.

THE JEWEL ROOM (Read Ephesians 4)

Here amid the flash of the Jewel Room, we will get our epaulets and our garments of holiness—"all lowliness and meekness, with long suffering." Here are our banners and escutcheons—"one Lord, one faith, one baptism." Here are the brilliant gems of the graces as we will take them—*But unto every one of us is given grace according to the measure of the gift of Christ.* (4:7) We must "put off," or lay aside, the old life as we would lay aside a garment, and "put on" the new life as a new garment. (4:22-25) We must be different, but how? In what respect? What are the things we should be very careful about? We must put away lying. Our speech shows our spirit. We must put away all bitterness and anger and harsh words. Be kind to each other. We must not have anything to do with deeds of darkness for we are children of light. Read all of Ephesians 4:31,32.

We must go into God's robing room, not to make the

garments but to put them on. God is the Tailor and He makes our dress to conform to our position and purpose in life. God wants His sons to wear suitable garments.

THE NEW MAN'S WALK

We have discovered as we have come into this Temple what our riches are in the heavenlies. (1:18-21) Now we must *walk worthy of the vocation wherewith ye are called*. (4:1) The way we live must correspond to our creed. A heavenly calling demands a heavenly conduct.

One man prayed, "Dear Jesus, I see now that Christians must be something more than merely orthodox, if the world is to be won. I see now that our churches will be filled if outsiders find that people in them love them. This draws sinners." This is what we must do if we are to attract our friends and acquaintances to Christ. This is not strange for the first thing they know about Christ is what they see in us.

When God puts upon us His jewels of grace, He seals us by His Spirit. (4:30) It is like a young man putting a diamond upon the engagement finger of one whom he has promised to marry. The Lord knoweth them that are His and we are sealed unto the day of redemption. The seal is the mark of ownership. "They are mine." When you have completed buying a piece of property the notary public stamps the deed with the government seal. Cattle on the range are branded and thus the owner is identified. The seal indicates guardianship. A seal is set for security. We are sealed until the day of redemption. Have you the seal? Show it then!

THE CHOIR AND ORATORY ROOM
(Read Ephesians 5)

In the Jewel Room we were bedecked as children of God and enjoined to walk worthy of our calling. We were sealed with the seal of ownership. Now we are to go out and be followers of God, as dear children. A Christian is "I" following Christ.

Speaking to yourselves in psalms and hymns and spiritual songs, singing and making melody in your heart to the Lord. (5:19) Sing, Christian, sing! Christ wants it so. A singing heart guarantees a transformed life. When the spirit fills the heart, the lips overflow with praise. We will walk the Christian life as we sing and talk about Christ.

Be not drunk with wine, wherein is excess; but be filled with the Spirit. (5:18)

The body, mind and spirit cannot function without outside stimulants. No one will think clearly or feel deeply unless something from without excites him. But this is where the tragedy comes. The world has plenty of powerful stimulants which give us quick and joyous reactions. But the results are devastating. Our bodies and minds are not made for such ruinous flames and are destroyed. Our bodies are for God's altars. *I beseech you therefore, brethren . . . that ye present your bodies a living sacrifice,* is God's plea. The Holy Spirit fires our bodies and spirits and sets them aglow but never destroys. Therefore "be not drunk with wine, (the wrong fire), but be filled (set aflame) with the Spirit." We can burn and never be consumed. We can live dangerously for God and never be in danger.

It is just as great a sin not to be filled with the Spirit of God as it is to be drunken with wine. Don't think that only ministers and missionaries need to be filled with His blessed Presence, but all! God's Spirit is waiting that He might fill His temples.

There is a sociability in this great music room of God's Temple. We find it in relationship to everyone.

A CHRISTIAN'S WALK SOCIALLY

The Lord not only tells us to walk carefully in the spiritual sphere of our lives but in every other field. How is your walk as a Christian before your family, your friends, and your acquaintances? God demands a walk worthy of Him every place and everywhere. He teaches that a child of God must, under all circumstances, be a living witness of the power of Christ in his life.

THE ARMORY (Read Ephesians 6)

Now we stand in a room hung with the whole armor of God. The armor is His, not ours! But He tells us to put it on. We must put on the whole of it if we will be safe.

The Christian's walk includes a warfare. Let us know the wiles of the forces marshalled against us!

You must come to Calvary for each piece of this wonderful armor. When we come and take it for ourselves, we can see that our whole body is covered. This armor is for defensive, not offensive, warfare. We are to *be able to stand against* the enemy. Stand, Christian, in the victory Christ wrought on Calvary. But you notice there is no armor for the back. The Christian is never supposed to run from his enemies but fight the good fight of faith, praying always! Keep in ceaseless communication with your Commander.

Minimum Daily Requirements / Spiritual Vitamins

Sunday: THE BELIEVER'S POSITION Ephesians 1:1-23
Monday: SAVED BY GRACE Ephesians 2:1-22
Tuesday: A MYSTERY REVEALED Ephesians 3:1-21
Wednesday: A CHRISTIAN'S WALK Ephesians 4:1-32
Thursday: FOLLOWING CHRIST Ephesians 5:1-20
Friday: LIVING WITH OTHERS Ephesians 5:21–6:9
Saturday: CHRISTIAN WARFARE Ephesians 6:10-24

Chapter 12

LET'S LOOK AT PHILIPPIANS

*PHILIPPIANS PORTRAYS JESUS CHRIST,
OUR JOY*

Finally, my brethren, rejoice in the Lord. (3:1)
Then there is a pause. Paul is trying to think of some
better last word to speak, but he can't find it. Presently
he cries, *And again I say—well—just rejoice, that is
enough.* (From Phil. 4:4)

Paul and Silas, you remember, sang in the jail there
at Philippi at midnight when their backs were bleeding
and sore! He is rejoicing now as he writes this letter,
chained to a Roman soldier, for he knows that his very
chains are helping him to spread the Gospel. He could
reach some in Caesar's household that he never could
otherwise have brought to Christ. He urged his

Philippian converts to rejoice because they were allowed to suffer for Christ. (1:29)

KEY WORD

The joy of the Lord is your strength. (Neh. 8:10) The word "joy," or "rejoice," occurs in this epistle sixteen times. Paul seems to laugh out loud for sheer joy in this epistle. He is the rejoicing apostle. "Joy" and "rejoice" and "all" are the words to underline. "Be glad" is Paul's exhortation.

JOY IN CHAINS

It hardly seems possible that Paul is writing from prison with chains holding him. His words seem to come from a light heart. It is evident that the soul of this great apostle is free! There is an atmosphere of joy even from prison. Paul's spirit is like the old colored man's at Colonel Clark's mission in Chicago. "Brethren," he said, "when I get to the gates of heaven, if they shut me out, I'll say, 'Anyhow I had a good time getting here.'"

This letter has no definite plan, but it is the sweetest of all Paul's letters. There is no scolding. It is more of a love letter which reveals the apostle's heart to this church which surpassed all the others in devotion.

JOY IN LIVING (Read Philippians 1)

Paul loved to call himself the servant (really "bond servant") of Jesus Christ. He had been made free by Christ but felt like the poor black slave girl who had been bought at the auction. Her buyer was a white man from the North who purchased her so he could set her free from her slave condition. After the bargain had been made, the man found it difficult to get the girl to realize she was actually free. At last it did dawn upon her what it all meant. Instead of rejoicing in her new found liberty, she fell at the feet of her deliverer, exclaiming, "Oh, he redeemed me! I will follow him. I can never thank him enough. I will serve him all my life." She would serve him out of a heart of love and gratitude. So it was with Paul. He had been set free from death and sin by the purchase price of Christ's blood and now he wanted to serve Him as long as he lived. He starts his epistle, "Paul, a slave of Jesus Christ." That is the reason he says, *For to me to live is Christ*.

You notice when Paul writes his letters he puts his name first. How sensible this is, for you know the first thing you do in opening a letter is to turn to the end and find out who wrote it.

PAUL PRAYS

Although in prison, Paul could pray for his friends. *I thank my God upon every remembrance of you, always in every prayer of mine for you all making request with joy, . . .* (1:3, 4)

Paul lived to intercede for others. So should every true Sunday school teacher, Christian friend, father, mother, brother, or sister remember others in their prayers without ceasing. Have you a "Prayer List"? Do you talk to the Lord about your friends? *Making request with joy*. Why can we rejoice in prayer? What is your answer?

MAKING PULPITS OUT OF TROUBLES

Although Paul was in prison, chained to a soldier, people came to hear him preach. The Roman guards were so interested in the Gospel that they spread it around. This encouraged others to be bold in preaching and many found Paul's Christ.

There is great power in the witness of a consistent life. You may be bound to unsympathetic companions, but by your life you may win them for God. Your obstacle may become your pulpit. The Christian who works for Christ when everything is against him stirs others up.

Dr. Hinson, the preacher, met one of his congregation on the street one day and asked him how he was. "All right under the circumstances," was the answer. "Where did you say you were?" asked the preacher. "I didn't say I was anywhere. I just said I was all right under the circumstances." "That's what I thought you said," was the quick reply. "No Christian should be under the circumstances, but on top of circumstances. Climb out from underneath and stand on top of them and make them your pulpit." Job used his circumstances for a pulpit. Paul used his, and Daniel used his! Don't let your troubles weigh you down, but as the birds use the weight of their wings as a lift so use your trials as instruments of flying.

CHRIST IN MY LIFE

For to me to live is Christ. (1:21) Can you say this? Is Christ everything to you? Do you live for Him? Is your one aim and purpose to glorify Him?

Listen to the cries of the men of this world. What are they? To the successful business man it is, "To me to live is wealth." To the scholar, it is, "To me to live is knowledge." To the soldier, it is, "To me to live is victory." To the young man, "To me to live is pleasure." To the man desirous of recognition, "To me to live is fame." To the high school student, "To me to live is recognition." So we could go on and listen to all the voices of the world, but one is heard over them all—"To me to live is not wealth, nor knowledge, not fame nor glory, but Christ. Christ first, last, midst all and always Christ."

124

PAUL SAYS

When I travel, it is on Christ's errands.
When I suffer, it is in Christ's service.
When I speak, the theme is Christ.
When I write, Christ fills my letters.

Young man or woman, what do you think is the ruling passion of your life? Fill this blank in carefully and prayerfully. It will tell you much about why you are living and for whom. "For me to live is.................
...."

JOY IN SERVICE (Read Philippians 2)

Paul gives us the wonderful Example of the Christian life that we may follow in His steps. We must imitate Him for although He is Lord of all He became servant to all! Paul urges the church to complete his happiness by living together in love and unity. Is there anything more Christlike for Christians to do? *Fulfill ye my joy, that ye be like-minded.* (2:2) This is not an easy thing to do. If each one keeps his heart in tune with God, he will be in tune with others. The church would be a great choir.

What is the most important social grace? Elegance of manners? The gift of saying agreeable things? No, it is courtesy of heart and not mere fashion. Moody says, "Strife is knocking others down; vainglory is setting oneself up." "Each counting other better than himself" is an astonishing phrase; in other words, "I am willing to be third."

This mind we have been describing is the "disposition" of Christ. (2:5-11) Paul says, "Have the mind of Christ," which is self-forgetting love. Although He was God, He humbled Himself. Not only did Christ take on Himself the form of man, but the form of a servant. Then He humbled Himself more. He who was Author of life became obedient unto death. But even more than this, He faced an ignominious death, "even the death of the cross." This must be our spirit. *For whosoever will save his life shall lose it: and whosoever will lose his life for my sake shall find it.* (Matt. 16:25)

Paul is practical as well as profound. He never leaves us in the clouds. He never separates knowledge from action. Christianity is both life and creed. The creed without the life amounts to little. After Paul has scaled the heights in Christ's exaltation, he has no idea of leaving us there. *Wherefore, my beloved, . . . work out your own salvation.* "Work out" means live out, not working for salvation but showing the works of salvation. God has a plan for each of our lives as He has for Jesus. We must live it out. It is an absolutely personal matter. No one can do it for you. God plants in our hearts salvation in Christ, great, divine, and wonderful to be lived out. Can you go about it without *fear and trembling?* Happy is the person who finds God's plan for his life and falls in with it.

Christian experience is not something that is going on around you but in you. *Christ liveth in me!*

JOY IN FELLOWSHIP (Read Philippians 3)

Paul tells the Philippians that the duty of every Christian is that he be joyful. A long faced Christian is the worst advertisement against Christianity. The world doesn't want a greater burden; it wants a light heart. How can a Christian be joyful in a world so full of sorrow? Paul tells us in the first verse—*Rejoice in the Lord.*

Saul of Tarsus, a man rich in religious background, had been a member of the strict Judaic sect of the Pharisees. He was an earnest searcher after truth and kept the law with such care that he could state, "touching the righteousness which is in the law, blameless." One day he met Christ and he records the complete change that he underwent in evaluating things. (3:4-9) He gladly sacrificed and counted the treasures of this world as nothing in comparison with Christ. He set a new standard of values. He had a new reason for life. Christ had stepped in between Paul and his old ideals and made him change the headings at the top of his ledger. He erased "gains" (credits) and wrote "loss" (debit). This was his choice in life.

When Paul met the Lord on the way to Damascus (Acts 9), his whole being was changed. His eyes were opened. He discovered in Christ a store of spiritual wealth which made him count all that he had as trash. (3:7)

Like the sailor, who must throw overboard his precious cargo in order to save his ship and his life, so we must throw over much that we have counted as dear when we meet Christ. We may have a good family, as Paul had. We may boast of a good education. We may always have attended church and Sunday school and lived a good moral life, but God tells us our righteousness is only as filthy rags in His sight. We need Christ's righteousness.

Here are some of the ambitions of Paul's heart. Mark these in your Bible.

That I may win Christ. (3:8)

That I may know Him. (3:10)

That I may know the power of His resurrection. (3:10)

That I may know the fellowship of His sufferings. (3:10)

That I may apprehend that for which also I am apprehended. (3:12)

That I may gain the prize of the high calling of God in Christ Jesus. (3:14)

JOY IN REWARDS (Read Philippians 4)

Rejoice in the Lord alway: and again I say, Rejoice. Let your moderation be known unto all men. The Lord is at hand. (4:4,5) This blessed hope of Christ's coming again casts its gracious influence over all of life. Paul prays that the Christian may have joy at all times and not be worried by cares.

Moody says of verse six:

"Be careful for nothing;

Be prayerful for everything;

Be thankful for anything!"

Minimum Daily Requirements / Spiritual Vitamins

Sunday: JOY TRIUMPHS OVER SUFFERING Philippians 1:1-30

Monday: JOY IN CHRIST Philippians 2:1-11

Tuesday: JOY IN SALVATION Philippians 2:12-30

Wednesday: JOY IN CHRIST'S RIGHTEOUSNESS Philippians 3:1-9

Thursday: JOY IN CHRIST'S WILL Philippians 3:10-21

Friday: JOY IN CHRIST'S STRENGTH Philippians 4:1-7

Saturday: JOY IN CHRIST'S PROVISION Philippians 4:8-23

Chapter 13

A QUICK LOOK
AT THE NEW TESTAMENT

MATTHEW THROUGH PHILIPPIANS

INFORMATION PLEASE

1. Which of the Gospels portrays the Manhood of Jesus?
   a. Matthew ....
   b. Luke ....
   c. John ....
2. In which Gospel is the plan of salvation best presented?
   a. Matthew ....
   b. Mark ....
   c. John ....
3. The Sermon on the Mount is stated at greater length in:
   a. Matthew ....
   b. Mark ....
   c. Luke ....
4. The genealogy of Jesus is given in:
   a. Matthew ....
   b. Mark ....
   c. Luke ....
   d. John ....

COMPLETION TEST

1. Matthew was written especially for the.......................
2. The only Gospel that tells the story of the wise men is.......................
3. The two greatest preachers in the Book of Acts whose names begin with "P" are....................................... and ....

4. The greatest event in the Book of Acts begins with "P" also. What is it?...

WHAT'S THE ANSWER?

1. Name five outstanding miracles of Jesus.

....

....

....

....

....

2. Name three persons with whom Jesus had a personal interview.

....

....

....

3. In which one of Paul's letters is the *Love Chapter* found? ....

4. How is Jesus portrayed in each of the four Gospels?

....

....

....

....

5. How is Jesus portrayed in each of the six of Paul's epistles we have studied so far?

Romans:...

I Corinthians:...

II Corinthians: ....

Galatians:...

Ephesians:..

Philippians:..

6. Why did Paul call the Galatians "foolish"?

a. Because they followed other leaders. ....

b. Because they turned back from their liberty in Christ to the bondage of the law. ....

c. Because they formed a new church. ....

130

7. A Christian's "works" count before God:
   a. For his salvation. ....
   b. For rewards. ....
   c. For escape from punishment. ....
8. Name the epistles of Paul in their order from Romans to Philippians.

WHAT DO YOU KNOW OF PAUL'S FRIENDS?

Dr. Luke
Barnabas
Silas
Aquila and Priscilla
John Mark

SEEING PAUL THROUGH OTHER EYES

Give an account of Paul as if:
a. Barnabas were giving it
b. The Galatians were giving it
c. Dr. Luke were writing it
d. The Philippians were telling it

DISCUSS PAUL'S WORK AS:

Tentmaker
Pioneer Traveler
Inspired Writer
Wonderful Preacher
Evangelist
Organizer of Churches
Supervisor of Churches
Great Teacher of Theology
A Worker of Miracles
A Distinguished Prisoner

MATTHEW . . . . .

1—Coming of the King
From what person was Christ traced?.....................
What kingly name is given to Christ?.........................

2—Proclamation of the Kingdom
Why is John the Baptist called "The Forerunner"?

....

In what sermon were the standards of the Kingdom stated? ....
To what was the Kingdom of Heaven likened? (Mat. 13) ....

3—Rejection of the King
Who are the rightful heirs of the Kingdom? (John 1:11) ....
What important institution is mentioned in Matthew? (Mat. 16:17,18)...
What was Peter's great confession?............................

4—Triumph of the King
How did the crowds acclaim Jesus as King? (Mat. 21) ....
When will the whole world acclaim Christ as King? (Mat. 25) ....
What was the inscription placed on Christ's cross?

....

What was Christ's supreme triumph?...........................
What was Christ's great commission?...........................
To whom is the Book of Matthew written?.......................
In Matthew, Jesus is portrayed as.................................
The great message of the book is...................................

MARK . . . . .

1—The Servant Prepared
Why is no genealogy given in Mark?............................
Why are there more miracles than parables in Mark?

....

What five steps are there in Jesus' preparation?.........

....

132

2—The Servant Working
Describe a Perfect Servant's Sabbath.......................
....
What do the following think of Christ? Pharisees?
Multitude? Disciples? Yourself?.................................
....

3—The Servant Rejected
How did the people accept the Servant?.....................
....
What was the attitude toward Christ of the outstand-
ing religious groups of that day?..............................
....
What is the great sin of the age?..............................

4—The Servant Exalted
What claim of Christ is omitted in Mark's great
commission? ....
What is the great Servant doing at the book's close?
....

To whom is the book of Mark written?......................
In Mark, Jesus is portrayed as.................................
The great message of the book is.............................

LUKE .....
1—The Preparation of the Son of Man
What beautiful story is told in Luke 1 and 2?............
....
To whom is Christ's genealogy traced? Why?............
....

2—The Ministry of the Son of Man
How was Christ received in His own home town?......
....

3—The Suffering of the Son of Man
On what occasion did Christ utter the words *My
body which is broken for you?*..................................
How did Peter let his Lord down?..............................
What lessons about salvation are taught by the
thieves on their crosses?...

4—The Victory of the Son of Man

What happened on the "Emmaus road"?........................
What was one conclusive proof of Christ's resurrection? (Luke 24)..
What great promise closes the Book of Luke?............

....

To whom is the Book of Luke written?............................
In Luke, Jesus is portrayed as..
The great message of the book is..

JOHN . . . . .

1—Public Ministry

What three persons had interviews with Christ?........

....

How did Christ claim to be God?................................
What was the greatest "sign" of His deity?................

2—Private Ministry

Whom does Christ promise to send when He leaves?

....

What was Christ's "new commandment"?................

3—Suffering and Death

What does Christ mean by *My hour has come*?
(John 18) ....
Describe the action of the twelve during the hours of
Christ's death. (John 18; 19)................................
What words of Christ on the cross are recorded here?

....

4—Victory Over Death

How were the grave clothes a proof of His resurrection? ....
How many times did Christ appear after the resurrection? ....
How did Christ remove Thomas' doubts?................

....

What were Christ's closing words in John?................

....

What is the purpose of the Book of John? (20:31) ....

....

In John, Jesus is portrayed as ....
The great message of the book is ....

ACTS . . . . .

1—Power for Witnessing

What is the missionary challenge of this book? ....

....

Who are the chief characters of the book? ....

....

When was the Church of Christ born? ....
Why was the Holy Spirit given? ....

2—Witnessing in Jerusalem

Did the early Church teach Communism? ....
What miracle is recorded here? ....
Who was the first Christian martyr? ....

3—Witnessing in Judea and Samaria

How did the Gospel reach the Samaritans and Ethiopians? ....
How did "Saul" become "Paul"? ....
To what people was Paul sent? ....
How did Peter break down race prejudice? ....

....

4—Witnessing in the Uttermost Part of the Earth

Where was the term "Christian" first used? ....
Name the first church missionaries. ....
What was the purpose of the second missionary journey? ....
Jesus is portrayed as ....
The message of the book is ....

A Few Keys to the Book of Acts:

Two outstanding persons: Peter, 1-12; Paul, 13-28.
Two outstanding places: Jerusalem, 1-12; Antioch, 13-18.

Two outstanding facts: Coming of the Spirit; founding of the Church.

Two outstanding factors in service: The Spirit of God; the Word of God.

ROMANS . . . . .

1—What We Are by Nature

What verdict did God pronounce upon the world?

....

Why was this verdict given? (Romans 3:19)..............

....

Give one definition of sin. ....

2—How to Become a Christian

What is God's plan of salvation?................................

What do we mean by justification?..............................

What did Christ give that Adam took away from us?

....

3—How to Live a Christian Life

What is the right way to live the Christian life?........

....

What little word gives the clue to defeat in Christian life? (See Romans 7.)..

What in the eighth chapter replaces the "self" of chapter seven? ....

4—How to Serve God

What great challenge to service does Paul give youth in Romans 12? ....

What are the four spheres of Christian service?..........

....

How is Jesus portrayed in the Book of Romans?............

....

What is the message of the book? ....

I CORINTHIANS . . . . .

1—Corrections in Christian Conduct

What caused division in the Corinthian church?........

....

What was Paul's cure for this division? ....

What did the Jews think of the cross?.........................
.........................The Greeks?...........................
How should we judge our own lives?...........................
Is our conscience always right?...........................
What did Paul say our attitude toward vice should
be? ....
Why should a Christian strive to keep his body
pure? ....
What is higher even than the law in determining a
Christian's conduct? ....

2—Instructions in Christian Conduct

Why were spiritual gifts given to Christians? ....
....
What is God's love chapter? ....
What are the three pillars of the Gospel?...........................
....
Why is it so important to believe in the resurrection?
....

How is Jesus portrayed in this book? ....
What is the message of the book? ....

II CORINTHIANS . . . . .

1—Paul's Ministry

What is the source of all Christian comfort? ....
Why did Paul have to become a boaster? What were
his recommendations? ....
Why was Paul triumphant through his suffering? ....
....
What is the reason for suffering in this life? ....
....

2—Liberal Giving

What should characterize all Christian giving?........
....
What is the first thing we must give to God? ....
Why can God ask us to give everything? ....

3—Paul's Apostleship
How did Paul answer his critics? ....

Why did not God remove Paul's "thorn in the flesh"? ....

What verse shows that Christ can satisfy? ....

How is Jesus portrayed in this book? ....

What is the message of the book? ....

GALATIANS .....

1—Paul Defends His Apostleship
State the Gospel in brief. ....

Who authorized Paul to become an apostle? ....

2—Paul Defends the Gospel
What one word describes our best effort at saving ourselves? ....

What one word describes our letting God's best effort save us? ....

What is the difference between Religion and the Gospel? ....

What was the purpose of law? ....

3—Paul Desires the Gospel be Applied
When a man is "free from the law," what should govern his conduct? ....

What is God's law for reaping a spiritual harvest? ....

....

How is Jesus portrayed in this book? ....

What is the message of the book? ....

EPHESIANS .....

1—The Ante-room
To what is the Church likened in Ephesians? ....

What part did the Father have in our salvation? The Son? The Spirit? ....

2—The Audience Chamber of the King
What does Paul say we were "in time past"? (2:11-13) ....

What does God make out of poor humanity? ....

How are we saved? (2:8,9) ....

3—The Throne Room

What mystery is revealed in Ephesians? (3:6) ....

....

What verse speaks of our riches in Christ? ....

4—The Jewel Room

How must a Christian act? ....

How does God mark those who are His own? ....

5—The Choir and Oratory Room

Describe a Christian's walk socially. ....

What gives a Christian real "high life"? ....

6—The Armory

What is the best offensive in spiritual warfare? ....

....

Where may the Christian's armor be obtained? Describe it. ....

How is Jesus portrayed in this book? ....

What is the message of this book? ....

PHILIPPIANS . . . . .

1—Joy in Living

What is the key word of this book? ....

What is the source of true joy? ....

What name does Paul like to give himself? ....

How did Paul state his purpose in living? ....

2—Joy in Service

How may we follow Christ's example? ....

What does Paul mean by "work out your own salvation"? ....

3—Joy in Fellowship

What made Paul change his standards in life? ....

....

What was the greatest quest of Paul's life? ....

Where is our real citizenship? ....

4—Joy in Rewards

Chapter 14

LET'S LOOK AT COLOSSIANS

COLOSSIANS PORTRAYS JESUS CHRIST,
OUR LIFE

The Gospel, by this time, had been brought to "all the world" (1:6), and had been "preached to every creature" (1:23). Thirty-two years after Christ's death, the Gospel had reached the whole Roman world. It only needed one generation to establish the Church as a worldwide fact.

THE DEEPER LIFE (Read Colossians 1)

Paul opens this letter as he opens so many: "We give thanks." (1:3) He rejoices in the good news from the brethren scattered abroad in the various churches which he founded.

Notice Paul's favorite words, "faith," "love," and "hope" (vs. 4,5), which he so often uses. He wants everyone to have faith in Christ, love toward others and hope of heaven.

Paul tells us the secret of the deeper life that we as Christians should have in Christ. Dig downward first, and become "grounded and settled" in Christ. (1:23) Send the taproot of your Christian faith down deep into His life, as the great oak sends its root into the heart of the earth. We find that storms may beat against the solid oak, but it stands fast, for it is rooted deep.

Send your roots down into Christ. The source of your life is in Him. The Japanese have a way of cutting the taproot of the trees of the forest and confining them in miniature gardens and flower pots. The tree gains its life from the little surface roots and only grows to a few feet in height. Every soul is stunted until it puts its taproot into God and begins to draw on Him.

Next Paul presents a glowing description of the mighty Christ, the Superior One. He is ALL IN ALL.

CHRIST IS ALL IN ALL
In His Deity—(1:15)
In Creation—(1:15,16)
In Pre-eminence—(1:18)
In Redemption—(1:20-22)
In Headship—(1:18; 2:14)
In His Church—(1:18; 2:19)
In His Indwelling Presence—(1:27)

We find in this first scene, that not only are we in Christ, but Christ is in us. *Christ in you, the hope of glory* (1:27). This is what it is to be a Christian; living in Him, this glorious, wonderful person, the Creator of this universe, in whom we have redemption.

THE HIGHER LIFE (Read Colossians 2)

As ye have therefore received Christ Jesus the Lord, so walk ye in Him: rooted and built up in Him (2:6,

7). Paul is always practical. Again he says, *Act out what you believe*. You commenced well. Go on as you have begun! We have received Christ and have been grounded and settled in Him. (1:23) Let us therefore walk in Him. Paul always wants our walk and life to correspond to our belief. It is sad when a Christian believes in Christ and acts like the Devil. No one will accept his profession as sincere. If we have received Christ, let us walk as He would have us. If we have been rooted in Him, let us grow up in Him. If we have been founded on Him, let us be builded up on Him. All of these are outward evidences of a changed heart, a new life.

"Walking" expresses life.

"Growing" exhibits an inner power.

"Building up" shows progress of character until the structure is complete.

We have to do a great deal more than just believe truths about Christ. We must receive Christ if we are to have life. We cannot earn it or purchase it. It is a free gift. (2:6) We are rooted in Christ. That means we draw our nourishment from Him. A plant cannot grow unless it is in touch with the life-giving soil. We are built up in Him. We have our foundation in Him. Every structure needs a foundation. All this must be in our experience if we would be built up. The Christian life is starting in Christ, and then growing in His grace and gifts. We must be as dependent on Christ for steadfastness of walk as we were for our assurance of salvation.

All the life we have as Christians is the life "in Him." Our life in Christ is a person-to-Person relation with Him.

This is the life—real and satisfying, eternal life. We find in this chapter that Christ is all-sufficient, for *in Him dwelleth all the fulness of the Godhead bodily*. This is a tremendous truth for us to grasp. In this Jesus, who walked on the earth, dwelt the whole Godhead. But more than this—in Him was all the fulness of the Godhead.

Our life must first be built downward, "rooted in Christ." Next we must build upward, *built up in Him, and stablished in the faith* (2:7), rearing a stately structure to His praise, and of course, wholly by His grace. This is the higher life.

Meteorologists tell us that about twenty-five miles up, there are jet streams in which there are practically no disturbances. The higher you go with the Lord, the steadier is your disposition, the less disturbing are temptations and the smoother are the events in your everyday life.

THE INNER LIFE (Read Colossians 3)

The building of our life cannot be only downward, "rooted in Christ," upward, "built up in Him," but our building must also be inward. Let us know that Christ is the believer's life. Many believe that Christ gave us life as one would put a living seed into a flower pot. The pot would hold a detached thing—life. But Christ is more than that. He, Himself is in the believer. The life that is in Christ is in the believer. The illustration He gives, *I am the vine, ye are the branches.*

We find that our new life in Christ makes us less interested in the things the world offers. We become "dead to the world." As the little chorus puts it, "One look at Jesus and He settled it all for me." We find ourselves "hid with Christ," and as we know Him we discover, one by one, the beauties of the Lord Jesus. *Mercies, kindness, humbleness of mind, meekness, long-suffering.* (3:12) *Let the word of Christ dwell in you richly* (3:16). It will make a difference. Others will recognize it.

The Brown family lived in a house that was an eyesore in the neighborhood. Weeds grew over the porch; the shades were always torn; the curtains were sagging and soiled. One day in passing by the house, we saw the grass cut; fresh white curtains were hung at the windows. The broken steps were mended. "When did the Browns move?" we asked. "Why, they haven't moved," answered our neighbor. "O, yes they have. The Browns don't live in that house any more. A new family has moved in. I haven't seen the people yet, but I know by the appearance that a new owner occupies the house." Our outward life will be different. Others will see Christ living in us.

Since we are "risen with Christ," we should seek those things which are above, and show to the best of our ability what is the goal of our lives.

For example, the submarine is made to travel under water. Yet, every submarine is equipped with an elaborate periscope by which it seeks those things which are above. It travels in the water, but the well-being of those in it depends on a knowledge of what is above.

We live in the world, but we must set our minds (affections) on things above, for we are citizens of a heavenly country.

After we receive our new life in Christ Jesus, then we must "put off" the old man and his deeds. (3:5-9) It should not be necessary to tell Christians that they must put off things that are more like the Devil than the Saviour!

Old leaves are pushed off by the new leaves as they begin to appear in the spring. This is what happens when we receive Christ—the new life pushes off the old works. Christ wants consistent Christian living and fellowship among His people. Our conduct should correspond to the Christ who is our life.

Paul admonishes us to destroy our old nature and "put off" all its vices. Read over Paul's black catalogue. There is immorality, impurity, passion, greed. Then there is passionate anger and wrath, and the many sins of speech. Let us give up these sins. It is possible in Christ.

Can you imagine how ridiculous you would look if, when you went to buy a new suit, you refused to take off the one you had on, but rather insisted that the new one should be tried on without "putting off" the old one! This is what many Christians do. They try to put the garment of a new life on over their old nature. It just doesn't fit. We must lay aside sin; then "put on" the new man.

A Christian's conduct is what men see you do. As clothes indicate what kind of a person you are—they tell whether you are careful or careless; they tell whether you are a soldier or civilian, a king or a commoner—so outward expression will show "whose you are, and whom you serve." (Acts 27:23)

Paul says the new Christian not only puts away, but puts on or adds to his life. Let us "put on" the excellences of this new life, such as tenderness, kindness, humility, patience, forgiveness and love. (3:12-14) Yes, these are the things with which we are to adorn ourselves. If we lived like this we would find Paradise on earth.

Do you remember how Luther Burbank took the little wild daisy and developed it into a bloom five to seven inches in diameter, and the little poppy developed into a blossom ten inches across? So our Christian graces must be cultivated and enlarged. Too often they perish for want of care. Too often the fruit of our lives looks only like the ordinary fruit of the world. We must grow into the full stature of the fulness of Christ. Every living thing grows toward the sky, but even the giant sequoia cannot grow up into it.

Set down all the commands given to you in this chapter. They are many.

Yes, *Christ is all, and in all.* (3:11) If Christ is not all in your life, He is nothing. No surer test can be given to any false teaching of today than this: "Where does it put Jesus Christ? Is He something in it, or is He all?"

If Christ is not Lord of all, He is not Lord at all.

A Christian heart is a singing heart. (3:16) Christ wants us to be taught in His Word, and then He wants us to express our joy in Him by singing hymns. Teaching of the Word and singing of songs is the best way to promote the growth of the Christian life. Let us do more of it today in our churches.

THE OUTWARD LIFE (Read Colossians 4)

This chapter introduces another phase of our life in Christ, the outward life. We found we must build within, cultivating the virtues of the new life in Christ. But there is something more. We want our new life to be seen and felt among others. *Walk in wisdom toward them that are without, redeeming the time.* (4:5) This is the way we present Christ to the world. Remember, Christians mean "little Christs." The life of Christ is not written only by authors like Farrar or Edersheim. It was not ended when the Gospels were completed.

Christ is living in us. His life is told today in living epistles that are known and read of all men. What is the Gospel according to you? Make Christ known by your life.

You as a Christian can pass on the power of God to others. You can be a transmitter. One man said, "I am an electric bulb. I cannot create light myself; I have no light in myself, but God puts me where He will and I glow by His power. Sometimes I am a high-powered light and sometimes a parking light. But I am His and He puts me where I can best serve."

"BOOK at a GLANCE"
Colossians

There is no value in these reviews unless you actually go to the text itself and read it! Read the verses, FILL IN the blanks. Give one-word answers.

DEEPER LIFE

1. A companion word to the word "settled." (1:23)....

....

2. What Paul calls himself..

3. Word used to describe how we should "walk." (1:10)

....

HIGHER LIFE

1. A companion word for the phrase "built up." (2:7)

....

2. A one-word warning against erroneous teachings. (2:8) ....

INNER LIFE

1. One word telling us where to set our affections.......

....

2. A word describing security, safety, and secrecy. (3:3) ....

3. Description of how a Christian should try to "do" all things. (3:23) ....

148

OUTWARD LIFE

1. What should be done with our time? (4:5)...............
....

2. What is the "seasoning" recommended by Paul for our speech? (4:6)...

3. Record the name of a famous doctor mentioned in this scene. ....

Minimum Daily Requirements / Spiritual Vitamins

Sunday: PAUL'S GREETING AND PRAYER Colossians 1:1-14

Monday: SEVEN SUPERIORITIES OF CHRIST Colossians 1:15-29

Tuesday: CHRIST EXALTED Philippians 2:1-16

Wednesday: COMPLETE IN CHRIST Colossians 2:1-19

Thursday: OLD AND NEW MAN Colossians 2:20–3:11

Friday: CHRISTIAN LIVING Colossians 3:12-25

Saturday: CHRISTIAN GRACES Colossians 4:1-18

Chapter 15

LET'S LOOK AT I THESSALONIANS

*I THESSALONIANS PORTRAYS JESUS CHRIST,
THE COMING ONE*

Paul, accompanied by Timothy and Silas, had spent
only three Sundays at Thessalonica, on his second
missionary journey, but during that time he had not
only founded a church, but had grounded it firmly in
the faith.

It is an unprecedented thing even in the ministry of
Paul, this establishment of a flourishing church in less
than a month. He preached to them for three Sabbath
days, although no doubt he continued his meetings
during these weeks. Paul's success in Thessalonica has
not been the usual experience of missionaries among
the heathen. Carey in India, Judson in Burma, Morrison

150

in China, Moffat in Africa waited each seven years for his first convert. But here, the Holy Spirit allowed Paul to reap a sudden harvest.

The main subject of the book is the Lord's personal coming again. It is the "blessed hope" of the Church. Let us find the outline of the book around this truth.

There should be nothing doubtful or divisive about this "blessed hope" of our Lord's return. No one can read the Word without finding it. Let us not quarrel with one another about so sweet a message as our Lord's "I will come again." The only dispute possible is with the Lord Himself. Let us rather be watchful, for we know not the day nor the hour when the Son of Man cometh.

CHRIST'S COMING—AN INSPIRATION TO YOUNG CHRISTIANS (Read I Thessalonians 1)

In Paul's greeting, he includes his fellow-workers, Silvanus (Silas) and Timothy. We can learn much from Paul. He knew the secret of friendship, that so many would like to possess. He loved people. The Bible tells us how to have friends. *He that hath friends must show himself friendly.* This is just what Paul did. He always acknowledged others in his service, and expressed appreciation of their part in every work done. His name is linked with his friends and associates. He never forgot them.

We give thanks to God always for you all, making mention of you in our prayers (1:2). Do we follow up our new converts as Paul did? Paul's converts were in more than a score of different cities, yet he carried them "all" in his heart and kept in touch with them.

Do you have a Prayer List? Do you pray for others by name? Do you "make mention" of your friends before God? If you find it difficult to speak to others about Christ, try speaking to Christ about others, and soon you will be speaking to others about Him. This is something all of us can do, even the most timid.

Are we realizing as Christians what we are in the world for? How seriously are we taking our task? Have we any evidence that we have been "approved of God" to be entrusted with the Gospel? Paul sets forth in this letter the intensity of his ministry; his willingness to die for his new converts; and his dealing with "each one."

Paul thanks God for this church. The beauty of this church did not consist of a gorgeous building of mortar and stone, but a people who are *in God the Father and in the Lord Jesus Christ.* (1:1) He is very pleased over the wonderful growth these young converts have made. He held them up as an example everywhere he went. (1:7) Already their zeal had made a profound impression all over Macedonia and Achaia (Greece), and everyone was talking about the wonderful way God had worked in this young, vigorous church at Thessalonica.

Ye were ensamples to all that believe. (1:7) This is what everyone in the world is looking for—Christians who live the Christian life, who act what they believe. This is just what the Thessalonians did. Nothing was mentioned of the financial condition of their "Annual Budget." But their faith in God was known everywhere. (1:8) Their missionary enthusiasm in sounding forth the Word of God had been felt all through Greece. They were what every church should be—an encouraging example to others.

CHRIST'S COMING—AN ENCOURAGEMENT TO THE FAITHFUL SERVANT (Read I Thessalonians 2)

What a man was Paul! He preached to please God and lived to convince men of the truth of his preaching. His conduct commended his preaching. He was not a flatterer, neither did he seek wealth. He came simply as a child, and as gentle as a nurse caring for little children. He was never idle, but toiled night and day. Giving them this example of his own life, he pleaded with them to make their daily lives worthy of the name Christian.

Paul urges *that ye would walk worthy of God.* (2:12) A Christian's walk is a Christian's life. An Indian pastor who was worried over the inconsistent lives among some of his flock, said to a missionary, "There is much crooked walk by those who make good talk." Our walk and our talk should be twins going along on the same trail.

WHICH ARE YOU?
Self-Pleaser
Men-Pleaser
God-Pleaser

Paul chose to please God. His life really counted before men, brought blessing to himself.

PAUL'S CROWN

Paul looked forward during these trying days to the *Lord Jesus Christ at His coming.* His greatest reward, after he has seen his wonderful Saviour's face, will be to present the young converts of his ministry to Christ, letting them share in the glory of His advent. They will be his *crown of rejoicing* (2:19,20).

CHRIST'S COMING—AN INCENTIVE TO LOVE AMONG CHRISTIANS (Read I Thessalonians 3:1–4:12)

This scene describes Paul's "labor of love" among the brethren. Paul was aware of the strain under which the members of the church at Thessalonica were living. He sent Timothy from Athens to encourage them under their bitter persecution and to see how they were getting along.

Timothy had brought back the good news of their "faith" and "love." This report filled Paul with unbounded joy. How glad Paul was to hear of their firm stand in the faith and to know that they thought kindly of him and his fellow-workers and longed to see them. In the midst of their persecution and suffering, Paul flashed the light of that wonderful day when they should be made perfect and unblameable, when they shall be changed in a moment, and be holy before God. (See 3:13)

The test of any hope that a man holds is what it does for him NOW. Paul told them that the coming of the Lord should be an incentive to

Paul urges personal purity, and a life that is consistent with their testimony. (4:1) This is the place where most Christians fail. Let us strive to have our lives beyond reproach. Our attitude toward each other should be one of love. You remember the two commandments Jesus gave. First, *Thou shalt love the Lord thy God,* and second, *thy neighbor as thyself.* Paul charges us to *abound in love one toward another.* (3:12; 4:9,10)

We discover that looking for His glorious appearing does not mean a life of idleness. (Read I Thess. 4:11, 12.) If we were expecting a loved one to return home after a long absence, we would not just sit down as the day of his return approached. Rather would we be busy getting everything ready, doing the things he wanted done. Can you imagine a mother waiting for her son to come home from the service, after being gone two years, just sitting down and letting everything go! She would be fixing up her son's room; she would be busy baking his favorite cake, and preparing his favorite food, as she listened for his footsteps. This is the true

Christian's attitude concerning our blessed Lord's return. Our lives should be filled with noble expectancy which makes us busy Christians.

CHRIST'S COMING—A COMFORT TO THE BEREAVED
(Read I Thessalonians 4:13-18)

A little band of Indian converts in northwest Canada came to a missionary with a strange request. "We are always hearing what God has done," they said. "Now tell us what He is going to do."

Where would you find an answer to that wise question? We have it in our Bibles. He shall come again! (4:16) If one of your best friends said he was coming to see you, you would not rest until you found out when he was coming and how. But our wonderful Lord and Saviour says He is coming and He will transform the whole world and glorify all humanity. Can it be possible that we would be less curious about His coming than we would be about the fleeting visit of an earthly friend?

There is so much in these few verses that end with, *Wherefore comfort one another with these words.* (4:18) There is comfort because of His sure return.

The Christians at Thessalonica were disturbed because of their mistaken ideas about Christ's coming. They were under the impression that Christ's coming was soon and they were worried as to what would happen to those who had died. What part would they have in His glorious coming and kingdom?

When Christ returns to earth, He will not come alone. Our loved ones who have fallen asleep in Christ "will God bring with Him." What a meeting that will be! Death does not end all. Parents and children, husbands and wives, loved ones and friends will be united. How anxious we are to know that "ours" will be in that happy throng.

The Lord Himself shall descend from heaven. (4:16) Christ does not say He is going to send the messenger of death to bring His bride (the Church) home. He is coming Himself for her! *This same Jesus, . . . shall so come in like manner as ye have seen Him go into heaven* (Acts 1:11). And *They shall see the Son of man coming in the clouds of heaven with power and great glory* (Matt. 24:30). What a marvelous hope this is in a world where we are hearing the thunderings of disaster around us, and the rumblings of an earthquake of uncertainty beneath us. *Look up, for your redemption draweth nigh!*

Those who have Christian loved ones who have died should not give way to undue sorrow when they lay them in the grave for they have a double assurance from Christ's Word. There is the hope that one day all the dead in Christ shall rise. And the additional assurance that He may come again at any time. When Christ comes, He will greet the believers who are dead first and bring them with Him. (4:13,14) When the archangel shall sound the trumpet call of God, announcing the Lord's coming, then *the dead in Christ shall rise first* to meet Him. Then those that are alive and remain shall be caught up in the clouds to share with them the glory of His coming, and to be forever with the Lord. And Paul says, *Wherefore comfort one another with these words* (4:18).

The second coming of Christ was the bright hope of the early Church. The greatest fact of the past is that Christ came the first time, as a man, and died on the cross to free us from the penalty of sin. The greatest fact of the future is that He is coming again, as a King, to free us from the presence of sin. This great truth not only gives us comfort, but inspires us to watchfulness. (Matt. 24:42)

Then we which are alive and remain shall be caught

up together with them in the clouds, to meet the Lord in the air. (4:17)

Paul assures us that all shall not die before He comes. *We shall not all sleep* [die], *but we shall all be changed, in a moment, in the twinkling of an eye, at the last trump.* (I Cor. 15:51,52) Then we shall be *caught up together with them.* What a host of redeemed souls there will be—*a multitude no man can number.*

And so shall we ever be with the Lord (I Thess. 4:17). Made like Him, we shall ever be with Him. He has gone to prepare a place for you. *I will come again, and receive you unto Myself* (John 14:3). Heaven is where Christ is now. There we will be. This is heaven's greatest honor conferred on mortals. This belongs to us. This is the order of these great events:

The Lord's descent from heaven.

The dead in Christ raised.

The living believers changed.

The whole company caught up to meet the Lord in the air.

CHRIST'S COMING—A CHALLENGE TO HOLY LIVING
(Read I Thessalonians 5)

Christ's second coming will be like the coming of a thief in the night or like the flood in Noah's time. The world will know nothing of His return. They scoff at the idea. But Jesus said there would be "signs" before His coming so that watchful believers may know when the time is drawing near. Over and over again Jesus had told them that His coming would be as a thief in the night. (Matt. 24:36,42; 25:13; Mark 13:32-37; Luke 12:40; 21:25-35) He warned His disciples to be ever on the watch. This should be their duty and their attitude. Christians need have no fear of that glorious day.

157

Don't fix dates! We should live watchful lives. We should not live lives of sleepy indulgence but of wakeful watching. (I Thess. 5:6) The hope of Christ's coming does not mean a life of idleness. Activity should be the theme of our lives as we find it in this chapter.

Have you ever thought of Paul as a human example of what it means to follow Christ? Paul was "as straight as a shingle" and "as clean as a hound's tooth." Paul could challenge a critical examination of his record as a Christian. Paul had a brilliant mind, and a highly cultured one. We are apt to say, "How hardly shall a brainy man remain loyal to his Maker!" But Paul humbly prostrated his wonderful intellect at the feet of his Master. The only explanation of such a life is that it was entirely yielded to Christ. You can't be perfect in this life, young people. But there is one thing you can do one hundred per cent. It is what Paul did. You can give yourselves totally and without reserve to the Master.

Be ye therefore ready also: for the Son of man cometh at an hour when ye think not. (Luke 12:40) Every morning when we rise we should say to ourselves, *Be ye ready for your Lord's return, for He may come today.* Every night our closing question should be, *Would I be ready for my Lord if He should come before I wake?* (I Thess. 3:12,13) Don't live to be ready to die, but live that you may be ready for Christ's coming! (5:4-8)

"Amen. Come, Lord Jesus."

"BOOK at a GLANCE"
I Thessalonians

Inspiration (1:1-10)

Three tenses of the Christian life are found in I Thess.
1:3. They are summed up in three phrases. Name them.

(1)........................... (Past); (2)........................(Present)

(3)..(Future).

Encouragement (2:1-20)

What three kinds of pleasers are found in this chapter?
Check which kind we should be. (1)...............................

(2).............................. (3)...............................

What is Paul's crown of rejoicing?...............................

Incentive (3:1–4:12)

To what four things should the coming of the Lord be
an incentive?

(1) .... (2) ....

(3) .... (4) ....

Comfort (4:13-18)

What is the great comfort of the Christian?...................

At Christ's coming, what happens to the "dead in
Christ"? ....

To the living?...............................

....

Challenge (5:1-28)

What should the attitude of a Christian be as he waits
for the coming of the Lord?...............................

Minimum Daily Requirements / Spiritual Vitamins

Sunday: CHRIST'S COMING AN INSPIRATION TO YOUNG CHRISTIANS I Thessalonians 1

Monday: CHRIST'S COMING AN ENCOURAGEMENT TO THE FAITHFUL SERVANT I Thessalonians 2

Tuesday: CHRIST'S COMING AN INCENTIVE TO LOVE AMONG CHRISTIANS I Thessalonians 3:1–4:12

Wednesday: CHRIST'S COMING A COMFORT TO THE BEREAVED I Thessalonians 4:13-18

Thursday: CHRIST'S COMING A CHALLENGE TO HOLY LIVING I Thessalonians 5

Friday: CHRIST'S SUDDEN COMING Matthew 24:1-27

Saturday: TRIBULATION DAYS Matthew 24:29-51

Chapter 16

LET'S LOOK AT II THESSALONIANS

II THESSALONIANS PORTRAYS JESUS CHRIST,
OUR RETURNING LORD

The second coming of Christ is mentioned 318 times
in 260 chapters of the New Testament. From this we see
how important this subject is. The "coming of Christ"
should be cleared up a bit in our minds. One day, Christ
will come to take away His bride, the Church. He will
not be seen of the world at that time, but those who are
His, including the dead in Christ, shall be "caught up" to
meet Him. This is the teaching of I Thessalonians. After
the tribulation for those left on the earth, Christ will
appear to the world, with His Church, to establish His
throne upon the earth.

This second letter was written almost immediately

after I Thessalonians. In addition to their trials and persecutions, the Thessalonian Christians were "shaken in mind" and "troubled" by deceivers who made some believe that they were already passing through the great tribulation and that *the day of the Lord was already here*. Paul tries to clear up the difficulty. Today, when war is threatening and sorrow seems to cover the earth, people think that they are in the end "tribulation" time, which Christ said would come. This second epistle to the Thessalonians is good for all to read, so that these errors in our thinking shall be cleared up.

The church at Thessalonica was carried away with the expectation of Christ's glorious return. Who can help but be thrilled when he thinks about His triumphant coming? But we must keep our feet on the ground. We haven't been given wings yet! We must mix calm thought with a burning hope. We must work while we wait, and pray as we watch, for there is much to do while Christ tarries.

The message here is something like our Lord's word to His disciples in Acts 1. You remember their eager question, *Lord, wilt Thou at this time restore the kingdom? Leave that with the Father,* Jesus in effect replied. *Do your day's work and wait. The kingdom is coming. That is true and glory will attend it. Therefore, keep watching and work while you wait.*

CHRIST'S COMING—COMFORT IN PERSECUTION
(Read II Thessalonians 1)

Many believe that Christ will not come to set up His kingdom till all the world is converted, but verses 7-12 of this first chapter seem to destroy this view. Read them carefully and you will find that the thing emphasized is that the coming of the Lord will be a terror for the disobedient. *When the Son of man cometh, shall He find faith on the earth?*

The world has never seen our Lord Jesus since it

crucified Him. He has been hidden from their view. But one day He will appear to the whole world. In I Thessalonians, chapter four, Paul says that at first Christ will descend from heaven and, with the shout of the archangel, the Church will be caught away to be forever with the Lord. At that time He will be seen only by His own. He is coming for His Church. Paul says, *For the Lord Himself shall descend from heaven with a shout, . . . and the dead in Christ shall rise first: then we which are alive and remain shall be caught up together with them in the clouds, to meet the Lord in the air: and so shall we ever be with the Lord* (I Thess. 4:16,17). Will you be among those whom Christ will catch up?

Here in II Thessalonians, Paul says He will appear to the world with the *angels of His power in flaming fire, taking vengeance on them that know not God.* (1:7,8) First He comes to take His own out of this world. They will be caught up to meet Him in the air. (I Thess. 4:17) Then He appears for judgment. (Jude 15) *For unto every one that hath shall be given, and he shall have abundance: but from him that hath not shall be taken away even that which he hath. And cast ye the unprofitable servant into outer darkness: there shall be weeping and gnashing of teeth* (Matt. 25:29-30). Christ is coming in the air for His saints, and later He is coming to the earth with His saints to set up His kingdom. *When the Son of man shall come in His glory, and all the holy angels with Him, then shall He sit upon the throne of His glory.* (Matt. 25:31) Then *the earth shall be filled with the knowledge of the glory of the Lord, as the waters cover the sea* (Hab. 2:14).

CHRIST'S COMING — INSTRUCTIONS FOR THOSE IN CONFUSION (Read II Thessalonians 2)

The Thessalonian Christians were suffering great persecution, and some of them had begun to think that they were passing through "the great tribulation" of which Christ spoke as the terrible time which should precede His coming and that the day of the Lord was already present. They were disturbed about the time of the Lord's coming and were entertaining wrong views as to the nearness of His return. This was unsettling their lives. The reason for this was that a forged letter and report, both supposed to have come from the apostle Paul, had confused the church and added fuel to the fire. (II Thess. 2:2) Jesus had told the disciples, *Take heed that no man lead you astray* (Matt. 24:4, A.R.V.).

The coming again of Christ to the earth is the great future event that the Church has looked forward to since Christ ascended from the Mount of Olives and the two men in white apparel said that this same Jesus would so come in like manner as He went into heaven. (See Acts 1:11.) Because of its greatness it has overshadowed all other events. It is "at hand" because it looms so big.

One day we traveled up the western highway to Mount Rainier. The morning of the day we arrived the air was clear. The vision was perfect. There was the majestic snow-covered mountain. It seemed so near that it would only be a few minutes until we would be climbing up its side. We ate our breakfast and started off in anticipation. We rode on and there it was, but we hadn't reached it. Every once in a while a low hill and a turn in the road would cut it off from our vision, but lo, again it would appear in all its glory. But we weren't there yet. For three hours we traveled. There it was the greatest thing on our horizon. Other things fell into insignificance in proportion to its grandeur and importance. Lunch time came and still we had not arrived, but it kept beckoning us on. Finally it was upon us. We were there! This is a picture of Christ's coming again in glory. It has loomed big on the horizon of every

Christian's life since the early Church. It is the "blessed hope" of the Church. His coming is "at hand" because it is the greatest future event, but it may not be immediate because God must finish His plan before Christ comes.

This scene deals with the manner of Christ's coming—the time and the place. Do not be anxious. God will take care of His own program of the ages. But know this—the *Man of Sin must be revealed* first, and the *mystery of iniquity* work itself out.

Have you ever visited the great Hoover Dam and viewed the ponderous wall holding back millions of acre-feet of water by its mighty presence? Can you imagine the destruction and awful disaster that would occur if all at once a great power would lift that wall and allow the waters which were piled up and restrained by its presence, to dash down over the country below, carrying houses and bridges, men and women, to a terrible destruction and death? This is what occurred in 1927 when the St. Francis Dam in California gave way, and for miles and mi˙ there was nothing but cataclysm and catastrophe.

This gives you a little idea of what will happen to this old world when all the Christians, who are God's wall of righteousness which He has built to hold back the forces of evil from doing their deadliest deeds, are caught away—*in a moment, in the twinkling of an eye.* There will be nothing left to hold back the wickedness of men. Then there will be an awful revelation of the real sin in the world, when there is no hindering by good men and women. Then the sin of man will appear in the Man of Sin, or "that wicked one" whom we call the Antichrist. *His coming is after the working of Satan with all power and signs and lying wonders.* (2:8,9) Wickedness is already at work, in secret, but the Holy Spirit at present restrains it somewhat, but

165

when He is removed the wickedness incarnate in the Man of Sin will appear. This Man of Sin, Christ will destroy by the breath of His lips when He comes in power and great glory. For at the coming of the Lord there will be great activity on the part of Satan. He will perform deceiving miracles. He will delude those who have never received Christ or loved the truth. (II Thess. 2:11)

The Man of Sin is the same as the Antichrist spoken of by Daniel the prophet, and by the Lord in Matthew 24:23,24. In Revelation 13:1 John tells about him.

The Antichrist is a counterfeit Christ. Satan in a last desperate effort will try to imitate Christ. The world would not have God's Man; now they must have Satan's man.

THE ANTICHRIST
"Christ's Counterfeit"

Will establish himself in Jerusalem . . . . Matt. 24:15
Will make war with the saints . . . . Rev. 13:7
Will be worshiped as God . . . . II Thess. 2:4
Will do signs and lying wonders . . . . II Thess. 2:9
Will work for only three and a half years . . . . . Rev. 13:5,6
Will be cast into the lake of fire at Christ's
  coming . . . . Rev. 19:20

Does Paul teach that the world is getting better? Is it true that the preaching of the Gospel is going to win the whole world for Christ? If so, has the Gospel failed? What is God's plan for this present age?

The Gospel has not failed. It is accomplishing just what Christ intended it should accomplish—the gathering out of the world of a people for His Name, the Church. On the other hand, there is this "mystery of lawlessness" working (2:7), a development of anarchy among all classes of society. Don't be disheartened. Paul gives us a picture of the state of the world at the close of this age when Christ shall come again. There will be a great departure from the faith. In fact Christ says when He comes shall He find faith on the earth. This is the picture of the Church preceding Christ's return—a falling away, a great apostasy. Does Christ really mean this? We should judge so from His description of the end days in Matthew 24:1-14,36-42.

When Christ returns, He will find Antichrist (the Man of Sin) carrying out his satanic plans. From the description of the Man of Sin in the Scriptures and his diabolical role of mighty works and lying wonders, we do not see how that and the millenial glory could exist together.

It is just as God said it would be. Indeed, the darkest clouds that are gathering are but harbingers of the golden day that is surely coming, when our Lord Himself shall return to take up the reins of government.

BEFORE "THE DAY OF THE LORD'S JUDGMENT"

The Lord's coming will be "sudden" but sudden does not necessarily mean "immediate." We are to wait anxiously for this time when the Lord will gather His children to Himself. Christ tells us always to be ready. The "day of the Lord" is "at hand" but it will not come until certain things take place. God always follows out a program. Paul warns the people against confusing the hope of Christ's coming for His Church, with the day of the Lord's judgment. Before this "day of the Lord's judgment," the following things must happen:

A Great Falling Away from the Faith

How true this is, in the day in which we are living! People are leaving *the faith which was once delivered unto the saints* (Jude 3), and *denying the Lord that bought them* with His own precious blood (II Peter 2:1), and crucifying the Lord afresh, and putting Him to shame (Heb. 6:6). The world acknowledges Christ to be a teacher, but not the Saviour. *Because iniquity shall abound, the love of many shall wax cold.* (Matt. 24:12) These are perilous times. Scoffers will arise and scoff at the idea of Christ's coming.

The "Lawless One" Must Be Revealed

He will be revealed before Christ appears to the world. But not until the Lord has caught up His own will the lawless one come into public view. (2:8) This "lawless one" is described in 2:4. He will oppose God; he has the title "Antichrist."

The Holy Spirit Is Taken Away The "Man of Sin" Will Open His Awful Campaign Against the Lord

When Christ comes, He will find Antichrist ruling with all power and signs and lying wonders. It will be a time marked with strong delusions. This is Paul's prediction of the Antichrist. "The sin of man has its final outcome in the Man of Sin." Read Matthew 24:24. He will be destroyed by Christ.

CHRIST'S COMING—PRACTICAL PREPARATION IN SERVICE (Read II Thessalonians 3)

The time of this glorious event is to be left with God. The delay in the Lord's coming gives us real opportunities for service. There are two wrong views of the Lord's coming that must be watched. Either we become restless and troubled because of having to wait so long, or grow idle because we know that when He comes, He will right every wrong and overthrow iniquity. But both of theses attitudes are wrong. We are not just to stand and wait, but rather have "our loins girded" for service, making ready for the glorious day when He shall come. Let us not abandon the work that Christ has given us to do and become engaged in material things.

Paul gives some instructions to the Thessalonians:

Stand fast—don't be influenced by false teaching.

Hold that which you have been taught—don't lose any of your foundation truth.

Comfort your hearts.

Establish yourselves in every good word and work.

Then Paul asks for their prayers. (3:1) His heart was burdened and he needed their fellowship. He had great confidence in their faith.

The hope of Christ's coming stimulates without exciting; sobers without depressing. It is a balancing doctrine.

Some thought, because Christ was coming, they would just withdraw from business and not work, claiming the right to be supported by the brethren who had money. Paul was very drastic in his dealing with these lazy fellows. The attitude on the part of these men was absolutely wrong, and he asked them to look to him for an example. He never ceased to labor while he was preaching to them. He laid down a great principle of life that *if any man will not work, neither shall he eat.* Any view of Christianity that makes a man neglect his work for his livelihood is not of God. Although Paul always advocated charity toward those who were in need, and spent much time in taking up offerings for the poor, yet he was very severe in condemning the able-bodied fellow who could but would not work. He forbade the Church to support these folks, and even urged them to withdraw fellowship from them. God never makes a beggar out of anyone, nor does He ever bless laziness.

"BOOK at a GLANCE"
II Thessalonians

Comfort (Ch. 1)

How did the Thessalonians bear their persecution? (1:4) ....

How does the coming of Christ affect the unsaved? (1:7-9) ....

Instruction (Ch. 2)

What fact caused the Thessalonians such confusion? (2:2) ....

What answer did Paul give to their confusion? (2:3)

....

Preparation (Ch. 3)

What two wrong views of the Lord's coming must be avoided? ....

What three things should we do while waiting? (3:5,13, 16) a.................... b.................... c....................

Minimum Daily Requirements / Spiritual Vitamins

Sunday: PAUL'S SALUTATIONS Eph. 1:1,2; Phil. 1:1-4; Col. 1:1-3; I Thess. 1:1-3; II Thess. 1:1-4

Monday: CHRIST'S COMING OUR COMFORT II Thess. 1:5-12

Tuesday: EVENTS PRECEDING CHRIST'S COMING II Thess. 2:1-12

Wednesday: AN APPEAL TO SOUND DOCTRINE II Thess. 2:13-17

Thursday: THE CLOSE OF THE AGE Matt. 24:13-31

Friday: WARNING TO THE WICKED CONCERNING HIS COMING Matt. 24:30,31; Mark 8:38; II Thess. 1:7, 8; Jude 14,15; Rev. 1:7

Saturday: CONSISTENT CHRISTIAN CONDUCT II Thess. 3:1-18

170

Chapter 17

LET'S LOOK AT I TIMOTHY

I TIMOTHY PORTRAYS JESUS CHRIST,
OUR TEACHER

When Paul came back to Lystra on his second missionary journey, he took Timothy as his companion. What a wonderful thing for so young a man! After long years of training under this mighty man of God, Timothy was left in charge of the important church at Ephesus. This brought the timid young man face to face with serious problems. Think of this inexperienced young fellow being left in that big church to take the place of a man like its founder, Paul! How unworthy he must have felt! How he leaned on the Apostle for advice and direction!

One of the things to remember about this time of the

early Church is that there were no church buildings. Groups of Christians met in homes. No churches were built until about 200 years after Paul's day, and not until Constantine put an end to the persecution of Christians. This meant that there would be hundreds of small congregations, each with its own pastor. These pastors were called "elders." (Acts 20:17) In these letters to Timothy they are called "bishops." (3:1) Timothy's work was with these various pastors. Remember, there were no seminaries to prepare leaders. Paul had to train his own men. But in spite of no buildings and no theological seminaries, and also in spite of continued persecution, the Church grew by leaps and bounds.

WARNING AGAINST FALSE TEACHING
(Read I Timothy 1)

Paul warns Timothy to *hold faith and a good conscience* because these save men from spiritual shipwreck. It is a thrilling sight to see a ship loosened from her moorings and plunging into the ocean. But it is a solemn sight too, considering the many storms she is likely to meet. If this is true of a ship, how much more so of a Christian starting out on the voyage of life.

Paul speaks plainly of some who, having put away faith and a good conscience, have caused spiritual shipwreck and are wrecked for two worlds. Let us pay heed to his warnings.

Even some who are brought up in Christian homes, rooted in the faith, may become spiritually proud and intellectually vain, and begin to drift away from their early convictions. They are just drifting hulks. "What do you believe?" They give the agnostic's reply, "I don't know." "What is your relation to Christ?" Again "I don't know." If you don't know where you are, you are in danger.

A ship after a voyage of 3,000 miles, was wrecked at the Bishop's Rock Lighthouse because the captain thought he was two miles off the rocks. But he really didn't know where he was. His mistake sent 342 men to the depths of the sea.

But ship captains are not the only people who lose their reckoning. Every day we find men and women who do not know where they are going. If you are one of these, stop stock-still until you find out where you are. You are running in a fog. The rocks of destruction are close by.

Nearly everyone who goes wrong begins in this way. A nail was driven carelessly in the pilot-house, near the compass, which deflected it a trifle, but the compass was not trustworthy to steer by, and a great ocean liner came near being lost.

A deflection of our conscience may be slight, but in the width of a life it makes a tremendous difference in our goal. Act with decision even in the smallest matters of duty. Keep your conscience true.

Paul's charge to Timothy included more than soundness in doctrine. He wanted soundness in life. Paul realized that a man can believe the Word of God completely, and yet live a life far from its truth. It is sad when one's life and one's belief are poles apart!

In this letter Paul says that the best way of fighting error is with a life that measures up to the standards set down in God's Word. Remember, many of us are the only Bibles others ever read. Christians have to live better than other men in this world if their testimony is to count. We either commend Christ to others by our lives, or we drive them away from Him. How often have we heard, "Well, if that's what Christianity does for a man, I don't want any of it!"

Paul wants Timothy to live a life that will vindicate the truth he preaches. He challenges him to be a good soldier of Jesus Christ. Timothy is charged to "fight the good warfare." (1:18) This presents the thought of a campaign and all the responsibilities of the officer in command.

Paul humbly declares: *This is a faithful saying, and worthy of all acceptation, that Christ Jesus came into the world to save sinners; of whom I am chief* (1:15).

A singer may feel that he has a very good voice but let him compare himself with a Caruso and he feels as if he could never sing again. The reason many people today do not have a sense of sin is because they are not near to Christ. Just to stand in Christ's presence is enough to make us feel condemned. Paul did not realize how sinful he was until he was brought face to face with his Lord and Saviour. He felt his miraculous conversion was intended to be an example of how God can save and use the chiefest of sinners. Read 1:2-15.

DIRECTIONS FOR THE CHURCH
(Read I Timothy 2; 3)

Remember when we pray that God *will have all men to be saved, and to come unto the knowledge of the truth, for there is one God, and one mediator between God and men.* (2:4,5). Paul makes it clear that when we pray for one we can go straight to God for him. We need no saint or virgin to approach near to God, only the One who gave Himself a ransom for all. Our blessed Lord Himself stands in God's presence pleading for us.

For there is one God, and one mediator between God and men, the man Christ Jesus. (I Tim. 2:5).

Finally, let all who pray be clean in conduct and pure in character. (2:8-10) Let us lift up "holy hands" when we pray. That means that we should not fill our lives with worthless pleasures or needless things that absorb, but come to the Lord with a heart that is cleansed. (I John 1:9)

When we think of church officers, we immediately think of the "official board." Paul tells us the kind of people that really ought to be on the church board. If the Church shall fulfill her mission of proclaiming the Gospel and praying for all, then she must be governed properly and know the real reason for her existence. There are two officers described, who shall direct the church, bishops and deacons. Paul outlines the requirement for both groups.

After Paul stated the excellence of the office of bishop or pastor, he states the qualifications of the pastor's life. We see he must be a man well balanced. Read I Timothy 3:1-11.

We find as we look this over that the pastor must be a man of blameless character, having only one living wife, not quarrelsome, not greedy for money. He must be a skillful teacher, and one who makes his own children obey. He must not be a new convert, lest his head be turned with pride. He must have a good reputation in his community. It is important that the church have the right leadership. Good pastors lead a church forward. How we need good and faithful shepherds today!

Paul shows us the need of Christian conduct in church. Church manners are a lost art in most places today. It makes a great deal of difference how we behave, for behavior reveals character. It is not "do-havior" but "be-havior" that counts. It is what we are that speaks so loudly that men cannot hear what we say. We preach every hour by what we are. The early Christians preached love by their actions. Men said, "Behold how they love one another."

Paul gives us a beautiful description of the Church and states her purpose. He tells you how you ought to *behave thyself in the house of God, which is the church of the living God, the pillar and ground of the truth.* (3:15) The Church upholds all truth in the sight of men. She is the only earthly institution to which Christ committed the preaching of the Gospel. She needs elders and deacons to carry out her program.

DIRECTIONS FOR THE PASTOR
(Read I Timothy 4; 5; 6)

Picture the young pastor Timothy awed by his instructor, the fifty-year-old Apostle Paul, as he says, *In the latter times some shall depart from the faith, giving heed to seducing spirits, and doctrines of the devil; speaking lies in hypocrisy . . . forbidding to marry, and commanding to abstain from meats, which God hath created to be received with thanksgiving of them which believe and know the truth. For every creature of God is good . . . For it is sanctified by the word of God and prayer. If thou put the brethren in remembrance of these things, thou shalt be a good minister.*

Lead a godly life. *Godliness is profitable* (4:8). Religion is an appeal to common sense. God says it pays. In one way, Christianity is a business. It asks us to get out our account books, to study the current prices, to consider the possibilities of profit and loss, and decide, *What shall it profit a man, if he shall gain the whole world, and lose his own soul?* Paul, after taking account, found what he had counted as "gain" was "loss."

Does it pay to invest in the Christian life? Does it pay from the standpoint of life right now? God says it does. Christ says, *Seek ye first the kingdom of God, and His righteousness; and all these things shall be added unto you.*

A noted Puritan once said that God had only one Son, and He made him a minister.

Paul says to the young minister and to those of you who may be ministers, "Don't think entirely in terms of the physical, how you can please your body." Everyone is thinking in terms of "having fun," of "doing things." The body must be fed, clothed, entertained and pleased! *Bodily exercise is profitable for some things,* says Paul, *but godliness is profitable both for this life and the life to come.* Start living for eternity!

Be an example in both word and deed, in your love, faith and purity. Carry conviction and command respect. In order to do this give much attention to your reading and preaching and teaching. The best way to combat any error is by reiterating the simple Gospel truth. The Bible itself will do the job, if only you give it a chance. *Give thyself wholly to them* (the Scriptures). If a man is to succeed in the ministry, he cannot afford to give an ounce of his strength to anything else. It demands the whole man, the whole time. Godliness does not starve real living. You will not become a "sissy" if you are good.

Take heed to thyself and to thy teaching. First a minister must be true to his own calling; then he can teach it to others.

The way a minister treats his flock is of vital importance. He must deal wisely and fairly with each one. The widow must be cared for. Elders must be honored and supported, but they must also be reproved, even in public, if they are found guilty, that others may be warned. In other words, sin can never "get by" in the Church, no matter who is guilty of that sin.

EXAM
Oral, Before God

Look up I Timothy 4:12. Kneel humbly before your Lord. Ask yourself: Am I an example in:

1. Word (conversation)
2. Ways (conduct)
3. Love (consecration)
4. Faith (conviction)
5. Purity (cleanness)

Add up your score. One out of five—AVERAGE; two out of five—FAIR; three out of five—EXCELLENT; four out of five—SUPERIOR; five out of five—UNHEARD OF! Your grade, in any case, is directly due to the work of grace in your heart.

Do you have any difficulty at any of these points? Have any of us made it harder for others to know Christ because of our failings? Let us so yield to Him that others will be led to know Him, and to love Him by our ministry to all who know us.

Fight the good fight of faith. (6:12) Christ makes His appeal to the heroic in a man or woman. The Christian life is not a thing to be entered into lightly. We will not be carried into heaven on flowery beds of ease. We must fight if we would be conquerors. But it is a "good fight." Our attitude toward our Captain is this: *Speak, Lord, for Thy servant heareth,* and *Lord, what wilt Thou have me to do?* This spirit is born of personal devotion to the great Captain of our Salvation. Let us be good soldiers of His cross!

HOW ABOUT THE MINISTRY?

Facts Show That the Christian Ministry Is the World's Highest Calling

√ The New Testament is clear in its call to the Christian ministry. (I Tim. 4:6-16)

√ History shows that some of the world's greatest men have been ministers—Augustine, Luther, Calvin, Wesley, Spurgeon.

√ Experience proves that the Christian ministry affords finest opportunities for doing good.

√ Winning men to Christ and to life in Him is the highest service.

    I'll consider God's will in this matter.

    ☐ Check Here

"BOOK at a GLANCE"
I Timothy

Warning (1:1-20)

According to Paul, how you behave is a direct result of what you ....

How did Paul rate himself? (1:15) ....

On the sea of life, how can you keep from shipwreck?

....

Directions for the Church (2; 3)

Why does man need a mediator in approaching God?

....

Four aspects in the life of church officers are reviewed here. Name them ....

....

Directions for the Pastor (4; 5; 6)

What does Paul say are some of the duties of a good minister? ....

....

What does real godliness consist of?..................................

....

Minimum Daily Requirements / Spiritual Vitamins

Sunday: PUT UP A GOOD FIGHT I Timothy 1:1-20

Monday: PRAY FOR ALL MEN I Timothy 2:1-15

Tuesday: THE OFFICIAL BOARD I Timothy 3:1-16

Wednesday: THE GOOD MINISTER OF JESUS CHRIST
    I Timothy 4:1-16

Thursday: A MINISTER'S TASK I Timothy 5:1-25

Friday: BRIEFING THE CHRISTIAN MINISTER I Timothy
    6:1-21

Saturday: THE WHOLE BOOK I Timothy 1:1–6:21

Chapter 18

LET'S LOOK AT II TIMOTHY

*II TIMOTHY PORTRAYS JESUS CHRIST,
OUR EXAMPLE*

ENDURE IN THE HOME (Read II Timothy 1)

We must first guard our testimony in the home, which is the training center of the Christian life. This is the hardest place to begin. So many young people today do not have a strong Christian influence in their homes. The Bible is not read. The family altar has never been erected.

Timothy had been reared in a sweet Christian home, with his mother Eunice and his grandmother Lois. Paul mentions these wonderful Christian women and commends Timothy for having had early training at a

181

consecrated hearth, *that from a child thou hast known the scriptures.* (3:15)

Paul calls Timothy his *son in the faith.* It seems clear that the youth was led to confess Christ by Paul during his first missionary journey. He was a Christian from childhood.

Timothy possessed fine qualities, but he had excellent training as well. He had a splendid reputation in his own church. He was the constant companion of the great Apostle Paul. He knew the Word of God and made use of it in his life and teachings. (3:14-16) He manifested a splendid spirit of unselfishness in his service. He was given great responsibilities by Paul. All this was instrumental in a large degree in his training. (II Tim. 1:3; 3:15; 4:6-12)

Timothy is addressed, "Man of God." What does that mean? Godliness comes from the Word and prayer. God speaking to us and our speaking to God. Manliness includes truth in the mind, love in the heart, and righteousness in the life. Manliness is due to godliness. The grace of God makes a man godly, and then proceeds to make him manly.

The key verse is II Timothy 1:13. *Hold fast the form of sound words, which thou hast heard of me, in faith and love which is in Christ Jesus.* Paul's life was characterized by an unceasing effort to guard in its purity the priceless treasure of the Christian faith. He wanted it kept untarnished. We live in a day when it is being said that deeds not doctrine count, but Paul's teaching was that conduct must be based on creed.

As a man thinketh . . . so is he. Wrong thinking makes for wrong acting. World War II was brought about by three men possessed with wrong creeds. These creeds soon became conduct, and thousands died to correct it.

How easy it is for us not to make use of our gifts

and natural endowments. How many lose all initiative. In the first letter (4:14) Paul says, *Neglect not the gift that is in thee,* and in the second letter (1:6), Paul writes, *Stir up the gift of God, which is in thee!* How about our gift? Have we ever let God tell us what it is? Cultivate whatever God has given. Remember everyone has some talent. To be sure, some have five talents, others two and others only one. But stir up the gift you have.

We find in this first scene one of the apostle's "I know's." It is a verse which gives us great assurance. *I know whom I have believed, and am persuaded that He is able to keep that which I have committed unto Him against that day.* (1:12) What is your persuasion? Will your answer come swift and strong as Paul's, *I am persuaded that He is able to keep that which I have committed unto Him against that day?* Make it very personal. Don't say, "I know in whom," as the verse is so often quoted, but "I know WHOM I have believed."

ENDURE IN THE FIELD (Read II Timothy 2)

We must *endure hardness, as a good soldier* away from home, in the school, in the office, in the place of business. This is our field of service and discipline. Here we are to stand the test as one who *needeth not to be ashamed.* It is easy to let down when we get away from those who know us and expect much of us.

A CHRISTIAN IS LIKENED TO

A faithful steward 2:2
A hardy soldier 2:3,4
An athlete 2:5
A farmer 2:6

Paul says as a faithful steward entrust the truths you have learned from him to reliable men who in turn will teach others. As a brave soldier endure hardships. A soldier does not become entangled with ordinary affairs, but is under the authority of his superior officer. He leaves his business and friends to serve in the army. Let that be our attitude. The athlete, too, must observe this if he will gain the wreath of victory. As the farmer is the first to enjoy the fruit of his harvest, so will it be with you. Avoid business entanglements that will keep you from rendering the best service. Watch, too, lest the comforts of life and the common enjoyments make us to love ease too well. We become weak instead of strong as those who endure hardness.

Paul urged the people to keep away from foolish discussion, for these only breed quarrels and a Christian should not quarrel (v. 24). Do not argue about the Christian life. Live it! Outlive the world—live better than they do—and they will soon listen to what you have to say. The best argument for Christ is a victorious life.

APPROVED UNTO GOD

Have you the degree A.U.G.? It is one of high honor. As one of God's workmen, do your utmost to gain God's approval.

Can you wear the "A.U.G." of "approved unto God"?

God gives us a "sure foundation" upon which to build our lives—the foundation laid of God. (2:19) *It standeth sure,* for that Rock is Christ. All who build on it are sealed for Him. This is the inscription: *The Lord knoweth them that are His.* It is wonderful to know that we are known personally by Him. This is not true of any other religion under heaven. In Christianity we are God's children and He knows every one of us. *The very hairs of your head are all numbered.* He calleth us by name.

ENDURE IN THE FIGHT (Read II Timothy 3)

There is one way to be strengthened against all the vices today. We find it in verses 14 through 17. The

Scripture will make us wise unto salvation. (3:15) Jesus met His temptation by the Word of God. We can do no better.

CATALOGUE OF 20TH CENTURY VICES
(II Tim. 3:1-9)

Lovers of themselves more than of God.

Covetous—men will do anything to gain possession of what they want.

Proud and boastful—pride fills the heart.

Blasphemers—taking God's name in vain.

Disobedient to parents—no respect today.

Unthankful—no gratitude.

Unholy men—caring not for God.

Without natural affection—mothers taking children's lives.

Truce-breakers—promises mean nothing.

Lovers of pleasure—pleasure-mad.

Having a form of godliness but no power—only source of power is the Gospel.

Two Mongol Tartar chiefs were engaged by a missionary to assist him in translating the Gospels into the language of their country. They had to study the subject intently. When the work was completed the book was closed on the table before them. They both sat serious and silent. At last the missionary asked them what was the matter. Surprised and delighted was he to hear both of them declare that they were ready to accept Christ. "We studied the sacred writings of the Chinese and the more we read the more obscure was the sense. But the longer we have read the Gospel, the more simple and intelligible it became, until at last it seemed as if Jesus were talking with us." Yes, the Scripture will make you wise unto salvation!

Have you ever heard anyone say, "I was a drunkard, a disgrace to my family, a nuisance to the world, until I began to study mathematics and learned the multiplication table, but since then I have been happy as the day is long. I feel like singing all the time, for my heart is at peace!" Have you ever heard a person ascribing his salvation from drunkenness and sin to the multiplication table or to science? Of course you haven't. But thousands have said, "I was unhappy and heartbroken. I had no reason for living until I heard God speak to me through His Word, and now I know a living Saviour."

The Word of God is the only thing that will keep the Church in this terrible day. The Church of Rome put aside the Word and the Dark Ages was the result. The Protestants brought it back into circulation, but Christians everywhere are neglecting it. The ignorance of the Word today is appalling.

ENDURE TO DEATH (Read II Timothy 4)

To endure to the end and look back over a hard and bitter fight and say, "I have won!"—that is enduring as a good soldier. Life's last hours for Paul were full of glory. He forgot that the lions in the arena, or the flames at the stake, or a cruel cross might end his earthly life at any moment. His good fight was ended, his long hard race was run, and now only the memories of a noble life gave him great peace.

One day a dispatch rider brought a long verbal message to the headquarters of an army at the front. He had to run the gauntlet of a heavy fire and on account of great risks he had to commit this message to memory. It took over half an hour to deliver, for it was as long as a lecture. At the end the officer taking it down said, "Now, is there anything else?" "Yes, sir," was the quiet answer, as though it didn't matter, "I think I've been hit." He was taken to a hospital but died on the way. Paul was as faithful to his calling.

He closes this letter with a solemn farewell charge to Timothy, before God and Christ, who will judge him and who soon will appear to spread the Gospel everywhere. *Preach the Word; be instant in season,* for a time is coming when men will not listen to sound teaching.

THE ATHLETE ENTHUSIAST OF TARSUS

The Wrestler

I have fought a good fight. This refers not to the soldier, but to the wrestler; not so much to actual warfare as to the athlete's contest in the arena, and the word "good" means "beautiful" or outwardly attractive. Paul had what athletes would call "good form."

The Runner

I have finished my course. Right to the very end Paul made progress, and we see from this the thoroughness needed for true Christian service.

The Trustee

I have kept the faith. This is another illustration and shows the fidelity of the great apostle.

Strenuous—thorough—faithful. This is the kind of life a servant of God should live. This is what is needed today.

The Victor's Garland

Henceforth there is laid up for me a crown of righteousness. Paul anticipated an honor greater than those of the conqueror in the Olympic Games. That victor would receive only the fading wreath of laurel or ivy. For a few short days his home town would celebrate but the shouting would soon die away. Christ's athlete was more to be envied. His victory meant a new door of service and fellowship with the Lord Himself.

PAUL'S VALEDICTORY

In chapter four, verses 7-8 we have the grandest utterance of the grandest mortal who ever lived. Where can we match Paul's words which he wrote from his dungeon to Timothy, his own true son in the faith? Let us picture the old battle-scarred hero of the cross, standing in the gloomy dungeon, loaded with chains, and looking up through the one opening in the roof of his cell through which only a tiny shaft of light could enter, but which reveals his countenance with the expression of perfect peace. His lips are moving, and we hear him say, *I have fought a good fight, I have finished my course, I have kept the faith: henceforth there is laid up for me a crown of righteousness, which the Lord, the righteous judge, shall give me at that day: and not to me only, but unto all them also that love His appearing.* (II Tim. 4:7,8)

Soon the executioner's axe would sever that noble head from that scarred body, and his soul would be borne away into the very bosom of his beloved Lord and Saviour. What a welcome he would have in heaven! No returning conqueror in Rome would ever have so triumphal a procession.

This day he looks back over a long hard struggle. His words speak of the athlete's struggle. Paul loved these metaphors, drawn from the games of the Greeks— games which were so swift, so strenuous, so exacting and severe.

The crown is for Paul, but it is also for us—*for all them that love His appearing.* You and I, whose achievements are so much less than Paul's, may yet be partakers of Paul's heaven. Wasn't it fine that the Apostle remembered you and me in those last words— or was it you he referred to as one of *them that love His appearing?* Jesus Christ is coming again to the world. He Himself has said it, therefore it is true. He has warned us to watch for His coming. Do you expect Him? Would you like to see Him come? Could He drop in upon you at any moment and find you glad to see Him? Are your habits of thought and action such that you would be pleased? Could He point to something you are doing and say, *Well done, good and faithful servant?* or would you have to hide your face in shame? Do you *love His appearing?*

Surely the "crown" which gleams before us should spur us on to a new diligence in service. Do we love His appearing?

Some people were discussing the question of death when one old lady said, "I am not looking for the undertaker but for the Uptaker."

The last verses of this letter give us a glimpse of the loneliness of this great wrestler and runner. Many were leaving him, under the stress of persecution. But *the Lord stood with me, and strengthened me; that by me the preaching might be fully known.* This is the secret of Paul's success. This is why he could fight a good fight and finish the course. His greatest opportunity seemed to be reserved for the end. He stood in Nero's courthouse, face to face with the "lion," as he designated him. (4:17) He was alone, as far as human help was concerned. The great basilica was crowded, and every eye was fastened on the forsaken old man at the bar. Did he quail? Was he afraid? No, indeed! He leaped to the height of the momentous occasion. He was not content in defending himself. That he did, but much more. To the multitude, curious and hostile, he told out clearly the Gospel of Christ, and all the Gentiles heard.

When in October 1879 Edison produced his incandescent lamp and it was talked about in the New York Herald, the president of Stevens Institute of Technology (at that time the leading technical college in the United

States) said, "Mr. Edison's so-called invention is a failure, and I pity him when I think of how the Herald has ruined his reputation with such absurd talk." Who was that president? I don't know, do you? But the "failures" brilliantly light the room in which I am writing!

"BOOK at a GLANCE"
II Timothy

Endure in the Home (1:1-18)

What great influence in Timothy's early life does Paul mention? ....

Study Paul's teaching about gifts (talents). Compare this with Christ's teaching in Mattehw 25.

Endure in the Field (2:1-26)

To what is a Christian servant likened?...........................
....

What "degree" should a Christian strive for?...................

Endure in the Fight (3:1-17)

Name what you think are five of the worst 20th Century vices ....

What verse clearly states the inspiration of Scripture?
....
....Commit it to memory.

Endure to Death (4:1-22)

Repeat Paul's great valedictory.

Name the terms that compare the Christian life with a wrestling match. ....
....

Minimum Daily Requirements / Spiritual Vitamins

Sunday: STIR UP THY GIFT II Timothy 1:1-9

Monday: HOLD FAST TO THE TRUTH II Timothy 1:10-18

Tuesday: ENDURE HARDNESS AS A SOLDIER II Timothy 2:1-15

Wednesday: FOLLOW RIGHTEOUSNESS II Timothy 2:16-26

Thursday: KNOW THE SCRIPTURES II Timothy 3:1-17

Friday: BE FAITHFUL TO THE END II Timothy 4:1-22

Saturday: RECEIVE A CROWN I Cor. 9:25; II Tim. 4:8; James 1:12; I Peter 5:4; Rev. 2:10; 3:11

Chapter 19

LET'S LOOK AT TITUS and PHILEMON

TITUS AND PHILEMON
PORTRAY JESUS CHRIST:
OUR PATTERN; OUR LORD AND MASTER

WORKS FOR CHURCH OFFICERS (Read Titus 1)

Paul presents himself in this scene as the "bond servant" of the Lord Jesus Christ, then as His apostle. Paul loves to call himself a bondslave of Christ. Another time he says of Christ, *whose I am and whom I serve*. It is terrible to be a slave in the abstract, but to be a slave in the concrete sense—yes, a slave of Jesus Christ, to be bought by Him—that is wonderful. It is a slavery of love.

"In grace," Spurgeon once said, "you can be under bonds yet not in bondage. I am in bonds of wedlock but I feel no bondage. On the contrary it is joy to be so bound." Paul was a Roman citizen, born free, ready to assert his freedom on any and every occasion, but he was the slave of Jesus Christ, and proud of that servitude.

Paul was in prison, and Nero sat on the throne, but there would come a time when people would call their dog Nero and their sons they would proudly name Paul!

Paul left Titus in Crete to superintend the work of the church organization there. He wished Titus to establish new centers and get the work started. One or two families would be enough to start a church.

How do you act at home? What kind of a Christian are you there? This is so often the test of your Christianity. It is the home-life that counts. The Christian household is the main evangelizing agency everywhere. When the home is Christian, the community is Christian. For this reason, the bishop and pastor are enjoined to set a good example before the people. He must rule his own children well, for he who cannot rule his own household well cannot rule the church of God. (I Tim. 3:5) He must be a man of moral courage and sympathy. He must be a good teacher, and encourage others in his teaching. Remember, practically all the religion you have is what you have at home and in the family circle.

The Creton churches were being upset by outside teachers who, for the sake of money, were working havoc in "whole houses." (1:11) This probably meant whole congregations for the early Church met in private homes. Paul calls these fellows "abominable" and "disobedient" (1:16) and said they must be stopped in their teaching. He demands severity in dealing with them. How much false teaching there is today everywhere! There are more cults and sects which men and women are starting, by which they make themselves rich. Follow the dozens of programs on the radio in the name of religion. It seems easy today, as in Paul's day, for every false teacher to get a hearing and a following. Why is this? Paul says we know not the truth. Men have "itching ears" and want to hear something new. They do not want a religion that costs them anything but their money.

A SURE FOUNDATION

During the California earthquake an old saint in San Francisco remained in her room joyously rocking back and forth in her chair, singing while all around her people were running in dread of death. After all was over someone asked her how she could have had such a feeling of joy. "Oh," replied the old saint, "I was so happy in the thought that my God was mighty enough to rock the world like that, while He held me securely in His hand. I did not have time to be frightened."

WORKS FOR CHURCH MEMBERS (Read Titus 2; 3)

Paul believed that doctrine must be expressed in life, and so he had a word to Titus about the aged (2:2,3), the youth (2:4-6) and the slaves (2:9,10). Let us know the demands of the school of grace:

Leave the old life.

Live the new life.

Look for that blessed hope and glorious appearing of Christ (2:11-13).

How essential that this be our foundation! Then can we *adorn the doctrine of God our Saviour in all things.* (2:10) To think that we in any way can adorn the wonderful Gospel by our lives! As we put a frame on a beautiful picture, to enhance its beauty and make it more conspicuous, so we must adorn and make more beautiful the Gospel of Christ. A king in his royal robes is more easily recognized as such, than one in ordinary clothing. How we can either make or mar the Gospel! What is the "Gospel according to you"? In all things show thyself a pattern of good works. (2:7) The test of fellowship is not warmth of devotion, but holiness of life. One cannot live on strong "feelings." Some mistake religious feeling for holiness and good thoughts for good conduct. All make this error. There is use and abuse in religious emotion.

Be so faithful in your attitudes and obligations of life that critics of your religion will be silenced. (2:8) Make others say, "If this is what Christ can do for you, there must be something to your religion."

Not that we are saved by good works, but we are saved unto good works. Paul says we are saved by His mercy (3:5) and justified by His grace (3:7). But because we have been saved at such a cost, we should show it by "good works."

"God our Saviour" did not save us as a result of our good works, but through His kindness and according to His mercy. He cleansed us by His blood and gave us a new life by His Holy Spirit.

Paul urges citizens of the heavenly kingdom to be good citizens of the country under whose flag they live. Every Christian should be submissive to rulers and authority. (3:1,2; Rom. 13:1-7; I Pet. 2:13-17) Again Paul tells us "to be ready to every good work." (3:1)

GOOD WORKS

Don't say anything of a person if you can't say something good, is a wonderful admonition to follow. Paul said it long ago. *Speak evil of no man.* Don't be quarrelsome. Show a gentle spirit in your dealing with others. It is well for us to remember that *we ourselves also were sometimes foolish*. Yes, we had all the faults we hate in others. It is well to remember that the things we criticize in others are very apt to be our own weaknesses. We like to call attention to these faults in others to take eyes off of ourselves. Try this test on yourself.

Avoid controversies and foolish discussions. They are always useless and futile. So often an argument only strengthens a person in what he believed before. Do all you can to correct a person, but if he persists in causing divisions among you, after warning him once or twice, have nothing more to say to him. Reject him. (3:10) Devote your time in doing good. Meet the needs of men. Help others to live useful lives.

PHILEMON

Christian love and forgiveness are given prominence in this book.

This book shows the power of the Gospel in winning a runaway thief and slave, and in changing a master's mind. This is a book in "applied Christianity." It is a text book of social service.

One would hardly guess that it was written in prison but for two uncomplaining references to it. Usually letters coming out of prison or from people in affliction or disappointment breathe the atmosphere of sorrow or depression. Not so, Paul's letters!

This bit of verse could well be on every desk.

The Writing Table

"Be present at this table, Lord,
Be here and everywhere adored;
Each letter bless, and let it be
A little messenger from Thee."

—Anonymous

Notice the courtesy and tactfulness of Paul's letter. One's letter writing can be a real service for God, if we make it so. Some who find it hard to speak to anyone about Christ can write about Him. Then, too, a letter is good for the one who receives it, for he has a chance to read and re-read and think it over. Use the pen in witnessing to your friends. Remember most that has been preserved to us of Paul's ministry has come through his epistles. What a heritage his letters are for all Christians today! In order to appreciate what God thought of correspondence see how many letters He kept for us in Holy Scripture.

Is God helping you in your correspondence? Is the Spirit of Christ in your letters? We will write letters, once we catch Paul's spirit. Perhaps we shall not always do the thing with pen and ink and paper. But each of us is writing a letter with his life. The letter is to the world about us. Some life letters go into the wastebasket about as fast as they are written, for they are dictated by the spirit of self. But the letters which live and bless the world are those whose keynote springs from the Spirit of Christ.

This letter is addressed to Colosse, to a man and his wife and presumably a son. A little meeting of Christians was held at their home. Paul gives us a beautiful picture of a Christian home in the time of the early Church. This family was the nucleus of that home-church and doubtless other believers in Colosse gathered there for worship. There were no church buildings till the time of Constantine. One of the causes for the spiritual decline today is the lack of *the church in thy house*. Is there one in your house? It begins around the family altar. House to house prayer meetings have done a vast amount of good. Open your home, if it is possible, for fellowship and prayer. It blesses the host and those entertained.

Paul was a wonderful student of human nature. The picture he conjures up, of himself as the bent and battered *prisoner of Jesus Christ* (v. 9), opens a well of sympathy in the heart of Philemon as he reads his friend's letter. Onesimus, whose name means "profitable," had robbed his master and run away to the big city Rome. In some way he fell in with the little band of Christians surrounding Paul and was converted. Paul sends the boy back to his master, with this friendly, personal note. He takes pleasure in playing with the fellow's name. The "unprofitable" servant now will be "profitable." Christ makes a man profitable to others. Christianity changes a man's value to his fellow men.

In approaching the main purpose of the letter, Paul does not blurt it out at once. He anticipates anger, and so he uses the finest tact. He admits that Onesimus had been good for nothing in the past, but playfully alludes to his name, hoping to put the reader into a favorable mood.

While Philemon's voice trembles, Mother Apphia is wiping her eyes on her apron, and son Archippus is clearing his throat. All three read on into the letter. Paul has his little joke and pun, and the faces of the trio break into smiles. Onesimus, meanwhile, nervously fumbles his cap back of the door, then breaks into a broad grin, and the tension is over.

My dearly beloved Philemon:

You remember how we worked together for the Church in your house. I thank God for your friendship and mention you in my prayers. I have heard how faithful you are to the followers of Christ. God bless you.

I am an old man now and a prisoner in Rome for the sake of Jesus Christ. I want to ask a favor of you not for myself but for another whom I have learned to love. I call him my son because he has been so kind to

*me here. He is Onesimus, your runaway slave, who
found out that I was a prisoner. He has done everything to help me, just as you would have done had you
been here. He took your place.*

*I would like to keep him with me always, but he
belongs to you. He ran away, but is going back, so I am
sending this letter by him. I feel sure you will receive
him as a Christian brother, rather than a servant. I
hope you will be as glad to see him as you would to see
me. Be good to him for my sake. If he owes you any
money, you can charge it to me.*

Paul's action with regard to Onesimus is an illustration of the Lord's work on behalf of the sinner. Paul
does not minimize the sin, but he pleads for forgiveness
for the sinner on the ground of his own merit in the
eyes of Philemon, his friend. More than that, he makes
himself personally responsible for the debts of
Onesimus. *Put that to mine account.* This is the message of the Gospel. For Christ bore our sins in His own
body on the tree. This is what Christ does—takes the
sinner's place.

The secret of the solution of the capital-labor problem lies in the love of Christ, such as undoubtedly
existed between Philemon and Onesimus after the slave
returned home.

This epistle gives a clear idea of the attitude of
Christianity to the social organization of the world. The
subject of the epistle is slavery, which was widespread
in that day. Christianity does not merely free the
slaves, but teaches them that they and their masters are
one in Christ. The position of the women in India is
very much like that of slavery in the Roman Empire. If
missionaries were to denounce existing customs, it
would result in revolution, but the preaching and
acceptance of Christ is the sure way of destroying all
such unchristian practices.

Has Christianity yet driven slavery from the world? Here began the abolition of slavery. This terrible menace has been vanquished wherever brotherly love of Christ has been shed abroad. But there are still portions of the world in which slavery is practiced. Sometimes it is disguised by other names, but wherever human life is sold, wherever forced labor is carried on, slavery exists. Christ came to save men from the slavery of sin. And He came to change their lives. It is certainly the will of God that slavery of all kinds be abolished from individual lives and from the world.

If Timothy or Tychicus took Paul's dictation of this letter, Paul took the stylus or quill and wrote in his big, nearsighted scrawl: *This is my own handwriting. I, Paul, promise to refund it—not to mention that you owe me, over and above, your very soul!* (Moffatt's Trans. v. 19)

"TWO BOOKS at a GLANCE"
Titus
Works for Church Officers (1:1-16)
How were the early churches started? ....
Discover what Paul meant when he talked of "men with itching ears." ....
Works for Church Members (2;3)
What two things did Paul say would help young people to have a good influence? (Titus 2:4-6)...........................
Mark in your Bible the five references to good works in the book.

Philemon
What is the outstanding lesson of this book?....................
....
....
What is the only way Christian brotherhood can be established in this world? (vs. 15-17)...............................
....
How did Onesimus become "profitable" in life as well as in name? ....

Minimum Daily Requirements / Spiritual Vitamins

Sunday: CHURCH OFFICERS Titus 1:1-9
Monday: CHURCH ENEMIES Titus 1:10-16
Tuesday: CHURCH INFLUENCE Titus 2:1-8
Wednesday: CHURCH RULE Titus 2:9-15
Thursday: CHURCH WORKS Titus 3:1-15
Friday: A CHRISTIAN GENTLEMAN Philemon 1–7
Saturday: A PRISONER'S PLEA Philemon 8–25

Hebrews 11
Now faith is the
assurance of the
things we hope for
being the proof of
things we do not

Chapter 20

LET'S LOOK AT HEBREWS

*HEBREWS PORTRAYS JESUS CHRIST,
OUR INTERCESSOR AT THE THRONE*

This book was written, first of all, to Jewish Christians, probably of Jerusalem, who were wavering in
their faith. Because of the taunts and jeers of their
persecutors, the Jewish Christians were beginning to
think they had lost everything, altar, priests, sacrifices,
by accepting Christianity. The Apostle proves that they
had only lost the shadow to be given the substance
(Jesus Christ).

INSTEAD OF LOSING ALL—
THEY HAD GAINED ALL

We Have:
- a great High Priest (4:14)
- an anchor of the soul (6:19)
- a High Priest on the throne (8:1)
- an enduring possession (10:34)
- an altar (13:10)

We have the "better" things of Christianity. (Mark the 13 "betters.")

Do we know the real difference between having Christ as a Saviour and as a Priest? Well, this book answers the question.

THE SUPERIORITY OF THE PERSON OF CHRIST
(Read Hebrews 1:1—4:13)

Nowhere are our Lord's deity and humanity so emphasized as in Hebrews 1 and 2. As our great High Priest, Christ is able to understand all our need, because He is perfect Man. He is "touched with the feeling of our infirmities." He is able to meet all our need, because He is perfect God. *He is able.*

Write down all that you find about Christ in Hebrews 1 and 2. If you knew nothing more about Him than you found in these two chapters, you would know much.

Two great truths are taken for granted—the existence of God, and that He reveals Himself to men. He revealed Himself before, *in time past,* by the prophets; *in these last days . . . by His Son.* The Bible records a series of stories of how God speaks to man and reveals His will and His plan to them. How marvelous to hear His only begotten Son speak! *Hear ye Him!* In Christ *all voices merge into one Voice.*

Remember, this letter is written to rectify the erroneous idea that the Christian Jews had lost some things because they had taken up Christianity. The letter is written to correct this misconception. Christianity is not "giving up" but "receiving," receiving the greatest gifts of life, in fact Life itself, for Christ is Life.

THE ARGUMENT FOR CHRISTIANITY

The Superiority of the Person of Jesus Christ
The Lord Jesus Christ is greater than any human leader (prophets). (1:1-3)

The Lord Jesus Christ is greater than angels. (1:4–2:18)
The Lord Jesus Christ is greater than Moses. (3:1-19)
The Lord Jesus Christ is greater than Joshua. (4:1-16)

When God wanted to save man from his sin, He did not send an angel, but His Son. God came not in the form of an angel but in the form of a man. He became Man to redeem man. He suffered as a man and died as a man that He might be our Redeemer. (2:10) Jesus tasted the bitterness of death for us, in order that He might render the Devil powerless, who has the power of death. He came up from the grave with the keys of hell and of death and no longer can the Devil lock any of us in death. Jesus came not to help angels but men.

Hebrews 4:12 shows the power of God's Word. Let the Word search and try you! Let God's Word have its proper place in your life. It searches out every motive and desire and purpose of your life, and helps you in evaluating them. Christ is the living Word of God. He is alive (quick) and powerful and all-wise and all-knowing. Let Him have His way!

THE SUPERIORITY OF THE PRIESTHOOD OF CHRIST
(Read Hebrews 4:14–10:18)

Here begins the main theme of this book.

Of a Better Covenant. (8:13)

A better covenant because it is based on better promises. These promises are written on the heart, not on tables of stone. (8:10)

Of a Better Tabernacle. (9:1-12)

Christ officiates in heaven. The tabernacle was of this world. The high priest entered into the holy of holies once a year, but Christ has entered into the heavenly sanctuary "once and for all." Christ's was not an annual redemption, but an eternal one.

Of a Better Sacrifice. (10:18)

He Himself is the sacrifice. He offered Himself as a lamb without blemish, to cleanse us. The sacrifices of the Old Testament were calves and goats. They could not take away sin. They were but the shadow. This Sacrifice needed to be offered only once.

Christ is called our High Priest. What does that mean? We are taught very plainly in the Word that sin has cut men off from God. No sinner can approach God. The way has been closed. In the Old Testament, a representative, the high priest, whom God appointed, could come into God's presence only once a year, after sacrifice for the sins of the people had been made. He must offer the blood of calves and goats not only for the sins of the people, but for his own sins, for he too was a sinner. He then would go into the holy place, then on beyond the veil into the holy of holies where the Ark of the Covenant rested. Over it was the mercy seat, and here God met man through the mediator, the high priest.

How can we approach God today? Christ has made that possible. He is our High Priest, our Representative before the Father. He entered into the heavenly sanctuary, God's presence, bearing the blood of His own sacrifice to cleanse us from our sins and to give to us eternal salvation. His blood had to be shed, for *without shedding of blood is no remission.* (9:22) *But this man, after he had offered one sacrifice for sins forever, sat down on the right hand of God.* (10:12) *It is finished,* he said on the cross. All His work of redemption had been completed, hence we see Him sitting. We find this picture of Christ often in Hebrews.

Christ did not have to die more than once. He offered Himself once and for all as an offering for sin. This is why we can come boldly unto the throne of grace, that we may obtain mercy and find grace to help in time of need. (4:14-16)

Our High Priest is at the right hand of the Father at this minute, making intercession for you and for me! (7:25; 8:1; 10:12) He has gone *to appear in the presence of God for us.* (9:24) This is why we can have boldness to enter into the holiest by the blood of Jesus, by a new and living way. (10:19,20) Avail yourself of this glorious privilege.

CHRIST'S GREAT APPEARINGS

In Hebrews 9, our Lord's three great appearings stand out in letters of light:

PAST—

On the cross—"Once in the end of the world hath He appeared to put away sin by the sacrifice of Himself." (9:26)

PRESENT—

At the right hand of the throne—"Now to appear in the presence of God for us." (9:24)

FUTURE—

In the clouds of glory—"Unto them that look for Him shall He appear the second time without sin unto salvation." (9:28)

Christ offered Himself as the sacrifice, a Lamb, without blemish or spot. The priest offered the lives of calves and goats, but they could not take away sin. This better Sacrifice had only to be offered once and for all. (10:10-18)

Since Christ has made this new and living way into the presence of the Father, let us come boldly to the throne of grace. The sin question is settled forever.

Christ's death is sufficient. God can now not only forgive us our sins, but cleanse us from sin.

"What can wash away my sin? Nothing but the blood of Jesus."

Let us not only approach the throne of grace, but let us *not neglect the assembling of ourselves together*. (10:25) There is nothing like Christian fellowship to make us grow. Mr. Moody visited a woman who had grown cold in her Christian life. She said she had not been able to come to church, but otherwise she could not understand what had happened to make her feel as she did about spiritual things. Without saying a word, Mr. Moody arose and lifted out a live coal from the grate and placed it on the hearth. In a few moments the glow was gone, and the coal was black. "I see it," she said. You cannot continue to glow in your Christian life alone. You need the warmth of fellowship with other Christians. This is a command to us.

THE SUPERIORITY OF THE LIFE IN CHRIST

From now on, the writer tells us the kind of a life we should live, because of Christ's work as High Priest for us. We know He is at the right hand of God and that He *ever maketh intercession for us*. When Christ finished His work of redemption on earth, He went to heaven to continue His work of intercession for us.

After one has accepted Christ, there are planes of Christian living. Some Christians live in the basement of Christian experience, merely inside the building, but where it is dark, dismal and gloomy. Others live on the ground floor. They leave the first foundations and go on. Some sunlight enters but their outlook is upon the circumstances about them. The others live up higher. Sunlight and warmth flood the rooms. The noise and attractions of the worldly street do not disturb them. The air is pure. The outlook is toward the blue skies and distant mountains. These live above the world, hid with Christ in God. It is in this high realm that God wishes us all to live continuously.

Let us look at a few men and women of God whose names are given in Hebrews 11, that lived with a high look. The Holy Spirit tells us the secret of each life is faith, yet it is not so much his or her faith as their reliance upon our faithful God. A woman became known as a person of faith. Very often people would ask her, "Are you the woman with the great faith?" She would reply, "I am not the woman with the great faith, but the woman with the little faith in a great God!"

The secret of Christian living is simply allowing Christ to meet our needs. Some say, "I have no faith; I can't believe." Yet we constantly place faith in our fellow men. You want to go to New York from San Francisco. You buy your ticket and get on the train. In the course of your journey a half-dozen engineers will guide your train. Without seeing them or knowing a thing about their ability, you trust your life to them. Faith is just trusting God, believing Him. There is nothing mysterious about faith. It is a simple act of the will. Either we will believe God, or we won't. We decide. It is as simple as turning an electric light switch. This is not a difficult, or baffling, or mysterious thing to do. And the result is light and power. When we decide to believe God absolutely, then supernatural life and power enter our lives. A miracle is wrought within us. One of the practical results of faith is that it makes weak men strong. (11:34)

To live in the Hall of Faith forever we need to do two things. First, like anyone entering a race, *lay aside every encumbrance*. Yield everything to Christ. Second, we are really to believe that Jesus is trustworthy. When we do we have given up the sin which so easily besets us—for that is the sin of unbelief. We give up that sin by *looking unto Jesus*. After we have surrendered our lives to Christ and laid aside the deadly sin of unbelief, we can *run the race set before us, looking unto Jesus*.

There is only one kind of human being in the world that can please God. Who is it? Hebrews 11:6. It is not what we do for God, but what God does for us that makes a life of power and strength. Our great God, rather than our great faith, is the thing to think most about. It is fashionable to be doubtful rather than sure about the great facts of God and Christ and salvation. Remember, this cannot please God.

The little words "let us" give us the clue to this new life in Christ.

CLUES TO A LIFE OF FAITH
"LET US"

Draw near 10:22
Hold fast 10:23
Consider one another.........................10:24
Persevere 10:25
Lay aside every weight and sin...............12:1
Run with patience.............................12:1
Endure manfully, looking unto Jesus.........12:2
Consider Jesus 12:3
Despise not chastening.....................12:5-13
Follow peace with all men...................12:14
Avoid bitterness 12:15
Be loving and hospitable...................13:1-4
Be established in doctrine....................13:9
Go forth 13:13
Offer the sacrifice of praise...............13:15

Dr. Haldeman tersely calls Hebrews 11 "the Westminster Abbey of the Royal Dead"—*dead unto the world and alive unto God.*

Have you ever been to Westminster Abbey, or Arlington Cemetery, or Mt. Vernon? If so, you will understand what people mean when they call this chapter "The Westminister Abbey of Faith." Just as these wonderful spots contain memorials of some of the greatest men of the English speaking world, so this chapter is a record of the great heroes of faith.

What is faith? Faith is believing what God says and trusting Him. The question is not, "Do we believe?" but "Whom do we believe?"

The belief which is a mere intellectual conviction has never yet saved a soul, but the belief which means the surrender of the whole life to Christ is the belief which brings salvation.

Two boys stood on the edge of a frozen pond. One said, "Bill, I believe it will hold us up." "Do you?" said the other. "Yes." "Then get on." "No," said the first, "I don't want to." "Then you don't believe it will hold your weight." He was right. If a man stands outside the finished work of Christ and says, "I believe that. I believe its philosophy. I believe it is enough to save a man," that man is never saved. To be saved he must stand on the finished work of Christ.

Because of the great company of witnesses on the bleachers watching from heaven, let us run the race of life God has set before us. As an athlete would, when he is preparing for a race, let us lay aside every sinful habit, and anything that would hinder us. (12:1,2)

TO RUN LIFE'S RACE...

Let us have patience..........................**12:1**
Endure chastening............................**12:11**
Follow peace and purity of heart...............**12:14**
Always look to Jesus, the author and finisher of our faith.

A life well pleasing in His sight will be made possible by the Lord Himself.

"BOOK at a GLANCE"
Hebrews—"Superiority"

Of the Person of Christ (1:1–4:13)
Discover the difference between the deity and the humanity of Christ.

List four great truths you have found about Christ.........

....

Name the four personalities to whom Christ is superior.

....

Of the Priesthood of Christ (4:14–10:18)
Christ is the Priest of a better........................., a better
........................., and a better........................
Define what is meant by the word priest........................

Of the Life in Christ (10:19–13:25)
Give God's definition of faith in Hebrews 11:1..............

....

Why is such great stress placed upon faith in the Christian life? ....

Minimum Daily Requirements / Spiritual Vitamins
Sunday: CHRIST SUPERIOR TO PROPHETS AND ANGELS
Hebrews 1:1-14

Monday: CHRIST SUPERIOR TO MOSES Hebrews 3:1-19

Tuesday: CHRIST SUPERIOR TO AARON Hebrews 5:1-14

Wednesday: CHRIST'S SUPERIOR COVENANTS Hebrews
8:1-13

Thursday: CHRIST'S SUPERIOR ATONEMENT Hebrews
10:1-25

Friday: CHRIST'S SUPERIOR FAITH LIFE Hebrews
11:1-40

Saturday: CHRIST'S SUPERIOR PRIVILEGES Hebrews
12:1–13:25

Chapter 21

LET'S LOOK AT JAMES

JAMES PORTRAYS JESUS CHRIST,
OUR PATTERN

FAITH VICTOR OVER TEMPTATION
(Read James 1:1-21)

Spiritual arithmetic is of value. The arithmetic of the
Bible is important and none of us can afford to ignore
it. James invites Christians to "count." *Count it all joy*
when ye fall into divers temptations (1:2). We usually
count it joy when we escape temptation and sorrow.
Instead we should count testing as a glorious opportunity of proving our faith, just as the automobile
manufacturer knows that the best proof of the car's
worth is the road test. Why we must count it joy is not
because of the trial itself but what it will work out. In

other words, use your trials. What is the purpose of the testing? (1:3) God makes our trials the instrument of blessing. Too often our trial works impatience, but God will give grace that His real purpose may be accomplished. Patience is more necessary than anything else in our faith life. When you can endure, you are a mature Christian.

Let us be careful where we lay the blame of temptation. Read 1:14 carefully. Testings of character come from God (Gen. 22:1), but temptations to evil never come from Him, but from the adversary through our own corrupt nature. (James 1:13) The appeal is made to meet a proper desire in an improper way. (1:14) Instead of wrong things coming from God, we find that only good and perfect gifts come from above, from the Father of lights, who never changes. (1:17) Our God is a God who loves to give. Alexander the Great said to one overwhelmed with his generosity, "I give as a king!" Jehovah gives as the infinite God.

When you are wronged and insulted ask God how you shall act. *If any of you lack wisdom, let him ask of God, that giveth to all men liberally, and upbraideth not; and it shall be given him* (1:5). What a sad lack! What a mess such a lack can lead us into. Does James say, "If you lack wisdom, sit down and think or study?" No, he says the wisdom we need is from above.

James begins and ends with prayer. (1:5-8; 5:13-18) Prayer is one of the easiest subjects to talk upon, but one of the hardest to practice. James had much to say about prayer. Find all you can on this subject in this epistle. What about his practice? Tradition tells us that on his death they discovered that his knees were worn hard as a camel's through constant habit of prayer.

FAITH SHOWN IN OUR ACTIONS
(Read James 1:22—2:26)

Don't be merely listeners of God's Word, but put the Gospel into practice. What is the good of a man saying that he has faith, if he does not prove it by actions? We must not be satisfied with only "hearing." We must go on doing. (1:22) If anyone is a hearer and not a doer, he is like a person looking at himself in a mirror and then going away and forgetting how he looked, or what was wrong—*straightway forgetteth what manner of man he was* (1:24).

Try this experiment to prove the truth of this statement. Look in a mirror and then turn away. Close your eyes and try to remember how you look. You can't picture yourself. Now try to recall how your best friend looks. It is easy to remember another face, but not your own. That is the reason James says we must keep looking into the mirror of God's Word to remember how we look, to find out the sin in our life. He who looks carefully into the Scriptures and practices them, will be blessed in what he does. If anyone thinks he is religious and bridles not his tongue, this man's religion is vain. The religion that does not influence the tongue is not a true or vital one. An uncontrolled tongue in a Christian is a terrible thing—guard it. Control your temper. It is dangerous. Under trial, be slow to speak. Keep the draft closed and the fire will go out. (1:26)

WHAT SHALL WE DO WITH THE WORD?

Receive it 1:21
Hear it 1:23
Do it 1:22
Examine it 1:25

Works do not save us, but they are a pretty good evidence that we are saved. *Inasmuch as ye have done it unto one of the least of these my brethren, ye have done it unto Me* (Matt. 25:40). is not a saving text, but a sign text. What He has done is our salvation. What *ye have done* is the proof of it. Keep faith and works in their proper place. Works are the fruit of your faith.

"I hear you are opposed to works," someone said to Spurgeon. "No, I am not," the great preacher replied, "nor to chimney pots, but I would not put them at the foundation." Let faith always come first. Faith without works is unseen of men, as works without faith is unseen of God.

Because of all this, James says in effect, "The faith you have is the faith you show." *Pure religion and undefiled before God and the Father is this, To visit the fatherless and widows in their affliction, and to keep himself unspotted from the world* (1:27). True religion produces a pure life, "unspotted from the world," and a useful life, "visit the fatherless and widows."

Christianity is a brotherhood that has no "respect of persons." (2:1-4)

James Russell Lowell once said, "We have gone on far too long on the principle, 'I am as good as you.' This is a principle of selfishness that has made the world sick almost unto death. We should act rather on the other principle, 'You are as good as I,' for this is the note of brotherhood and of humility, which the Lord and His apostles first declared unto men." (2:1-13)

How the world today ignores James' command not to have respect to persons! The world worships the successful, strong and wealthy, and despises the man who is poor. A Christian must not show partiality to the man of wealth and position, James tells us, but it seems that money and honor are the only things that men worship today.

To disobey God's law is sin. It is human to gloss over sin. A little girl said when excusing herself for something she had done, "I haven't broken the commandment; I have only cracked it." James says that whosoever obeys the whole law, and only makes a single slip, is guilty of everything. (2:10,11) He is a lawbreaker. If a man is brought into court for violating a traffic ordinance, he does not plead that he has kept all the others. The judge is only interested in the fact of whether he has broken this one with which he is charged. That classifies him as a lawbreaker. We may have a fine chain, but of what use is it if all the links are good except one? That broken link renders the entire chain useless.

It is clear that the one sin thought of here is mentioned in 2:9—"respect of persons." There are few, who if left to themselves would ever dream of reckoning such behavior as sin.

"Faith and works" are like two oars on a boat. If you pulled with just one, the boat would move round and round. You must pull on both to go forward. So faith without works, or works without faith, will not suffice to bring us into our desired haven. But let there be both, and the haven will be safely reached. Just as a body without a spirit is dead, so faith is dead without actions. (2:17)

FAITH SHOWN IN OUR WORDS
(Read James 3:1-18)

Our speech reveals what and whose we are. It expresses our personality more than anything else.

Anyone who controls his tongue, James says, is a perfect man. (3:2) If he has mastery over that difficult member, the tongue, the rest is easy. He is able to curb the whole nature. Just as we control a spirited horse by a firm hand on the bridle, so the hand of the Man, Christ Jesus, can grip and firmly use the bit and bridle on our tongues. Even as a great ship is controlled by a very small rudder and turned in any direction the captain determines, so the pierced hand of Jesus can firmly control and wisely use the helm of our lives— our tongue. The tongue, though small, is very powerful. It can determine the course of human life.

THE TONGUE A DANGEROUS WEAPON

A fire as from hell (3:6)
A world of iniquity (3:6)
Full of deadly poison (3:8)
Unruly evil (3:8)
Untameable (3:7,8)

A single spark can set fire to a whole forest. A signboard in Pennsylvania showed a lighted match dropping into dry undergrowth. Above were the words "The Forest's Prime Evil." What it took centuries to grow, the match could burn down in a few hours. Life's prime evil is the matchstick of the tongue. What has taken years to build is torn down in a few minutes by an unruly tongue. It sets all the affairs of life on fire, for it is set on fire of hell itself. (3:6) Wild beasts can be tamed, but no one can tame the tongue. (3:7,8) Beware of the sins of the tongue. They are many—lying, swearing, gossiping and slandering.

A woman one day came to her minister in tears, and told of a story she had started, about a person which had made her move out of the community. Now she had found the tale was false. She would do anything to take back her words. "Go to the top of the steeple," he said, "and take a feather pillow with you. Scatter the feathers far and wide and then come down and gather up every feather." Of course he asked the impossible. Just so it is impossible for us to take back the words which we so carelessly send forth.

Remember, this same tongue can be used to testify for Christ and praise His holy name. It is the instrument that the Holy Spirit uses to magnify the Lord. (3:9,10) We ought not to praise God and curse men who are made in His likeness! Cruel words have wrecked homes, broken friendships, divided churches, and sent untold millions to ruin and despair. There are so many people who call themselves Christians who seem not to make the slightest effort to control the tongue.

It is a striking fact that you can tell by one leaf of a tree what the tree is. Every leaf tells the form and character of the tree to which it belongs. A little word or deed will often reveal a whole character. One hasty uncharitable act shows a heart not right with God.

FAITH SHOWN IN OUR PURITY OF CHARACTER
(Read James 4:1-17)

The Devil has organized this world system upon principles opposed to God in every way. They are principles of force, greed, ambition, selfishness and pleasure. The believer should be crucified to this world. (Gal. 6:14) We should count its passing pleasures, its honors, its treasures as of little value, and remain unmoved by its attractions. The world is that system of things about us, or that spirit within us, which is blind and deaf to the value of spiritual things and cares nothing about doing the will of God. Because we live in the world, surrounded by all its attractions and the things needful to our daily living, we must be very watchful to keep our affections above the border line of the world. (James 4:4)

Men keep asking, "How can we end war?" But James goes back farther and tells us what causes war. A cause of most of the wars which have devastated the earth has been some nation's desire to get what does not belong to them. This has always been the cause of quarrels between individuals. Selfishness is the root of it all. Next, men fail either to pray at all or else they pray with a wrong motive—to spend what they get upon themselves instead of having their lives glorify God.

(4:1-3) God promises to answer prayer, but He will not give to those who would consume it on their own pleasures. We see world-minded Christians praying for purely selfish reasons. So often you hear people say, "I don't believe in prayer. I prayed for a new car, and God didn't give it to me," or "My husband was sick and I prayed that God would heal him, and he died." In either case the answer might easily have led the person farther away from God. The car would have been used to carry him to the beach and not to church. The family circle restored could make the wife find her joy in her husband rather than in her Lord.

To be friends with the world means to be at enmity with God. (4:4) Jesus said, *Ye cannot serve God and mammon* (Matt. 6:24). Therefore surrender yourself to God, and be not subject to the Devil. When the Devil is resisted by those who have surrendered themselves to God, he flees.

FAITH SHOWN BY OUR PRAYER LIFE
(Read James 5:1-20)

Evidently many of the humble folk among the Christian Jews were being oppressed by the rich and their hard earnings were being *kept back by fraud* (5:4). James warns the rich! *Ye have heaped treasure together for the last days* (5:3). How true this is today—heaped up millions, yes, billions. The coffers of the rich are full indeed. They are charged with fraud, voluptuousness and injustice. How much goes on today under the cloak of Christianity! It is true there are some great Christian souls among the rich, but for the most part, James' picture of wealth holds good. You remember that Jesus said it was easier for a camel to go through the eye of a needle than for a rich man to enter heaven. When Jesus told the rich young man to go and sell all that he had and give it to the poor, if he wished eternal life, it is said of him, *He went away sorrowful, for he had great possessions.*

What hope is set before the oppressed laboring man of James' day? (5:7,8) How much better than the strike or the boycott! If the rich are at fault today, are not the poor equally so, if God's Word is the judge? The poor he advises to "be patient." (5:7) This is wise advice. But why be patient? The Lord will come and all wrongs will be righted and each will receive full measure for his labors.

Here again the tongue is brought in. It is amazing how many Christians, in ordinary conversation, take the name of the Lord in vain. (5:12) God says, *The Lord will not hold him guiltless that taketh His name in vain.* This is a serious indictment.

PRAYER SCHEDULE

Pray when in trouble.........................5:13
Pray when happy 5:13
Pray when sick...........................5:14,16
Pray when at fault........................5:16

This epistle closes abruptly on a high plane. It is with the gracious act of a Christian who finds someone erring from the truth, and converts him. Although only God can save a soul, He uses human instruments to accomplish it. That one, *shall save a soul from death, and shall hide a multitude of sins* (5:20).

"BOOK at a GLANCE"
James

Faith in Temptation (1:1-21)

Why does God allow a man to be tested?...........................

Faith in Actions (1:22–2:26)

What should be a Christian's attitude toward the poor?

Why do we consider faith that shows no works dead?

....

Faith in Words (3:1-18)
Whom does James call a perfect man?.............................
To what is the tongue likened?......................................

Faith in Purity (4:1-17)
What causes war?..
Why are our prayers not answered?...............................
What should the Christian's attitude be toward the whole
world system? ....

Faith in Prayer (5:1-20)
What command is given to the ungodly rich?.................

....

State a prayer promise given in James 5. ....

....

Minimum Daily Requirements / Spiritual Vitamins
Sunday: FAITH TESTED James 1:1-21
Monday: FAITH LIVED OUT James 1:22-27
Tuesday: FAITH AND BROTHERHOOD James 2:1-13
Wednesday: FAITH DEAD WITHOUT WORKS James
            2:14-26
Thursday: FAITH AND TONGUE CONTROL James 3:1-18
Friday: FAITH REBUKES WORLDLINESS James 4:1-17
Saturday: FAITH IN PRAYER James 5:1-20

Chapter 22

LET'S LOOK AT I PETER

I PETER PORTRAYS JESUS CHRIST,
PRECIOUS CORNERSTONE OF OUR FAITH

SEVEN PRECIOUS THINGS

Mark these in your Bible

Peter realized that in Christ he possessed a chest of precious gems. He spreads them out before us and tells us their value.

The picture of Peter in the Gospels is amazingly different from that found in his own writings. In the Gospels we see Peter, the impulsive, restless soul, sometimes fearless but again a coward, even going so far as to deny his Lord with a curse! In his own epistles, we see him patient, restful, and loving, with a courage purified and strengthened by the indwelling Spirit. This is a wonderful illustration of the transforming work of God in a human life.

PRIVILEGES OF THE CHRISTIAN
(Read I Peter 1:1–2:10)

What are our privileges as Christians? First, we are *redeemed by the precious blood of Christ.* This is our position in Christ. (1:18,19) Because of this relationship to Christ, we have everything in Him which God desires us to possess. If God has given us His Son, *will He not freely with Him give us all things?* If a young man gives a young lady a beautiful diamond ring, will he not be willing to give her the box in which it comes? So God has given us all things in Christ. Peter tells us of these in this letter.

ALL THIS AND HEAVEN TOO!

We have been begotten by Jesus Christ into a lively hope. 1:3

We have in reserve an incorruptible inheritance. 1:4,5,10

We are kept by the power of God. 1:5

We are being purified to fit us to stand with Christ. 1:7

We have salvation for our souls. 1:9

We have a Gospel the angels desire to look into. 1:12

We have a great hope. 1:13

We have redemption through His blood. 1:18,19

We shall not be confounded (ashamed). 2:6

We are born again by His Word. 1:23

We are built up a spiritual house. 2:5

We are a chosen people. 2:9

We shall have a crown of glory. 5:4

The secret of the life of a lovely young girl who was always beautiful in a home where none of her family knew Christ, was discovered when she died. Around her neck she had always worn a locket, which she said contained her lover's picture. Friends had often wished that they might see what was in it. When they opened it, there was no picture there but these words, *Whom having not seen, we love*. Let I Peter 1:8 be the secret of your life and its constant inspiration!

Peter gives good plain advice on how we ought to live. Here he says, *Gird up the loins of your mind, be sober, and hope to the end* (1:13). Fashion your life after the Lord Jesus Christ. Don't live your life after the old pattern. *Be ye holy; for I am holy*. Love one another (1:22). Seeing you are "born again" (1:23), live like it. You are a new creature in Christ Jesus.

How can anyone *put away all wickedness*, as Peter commands? (Chapter 2) Not by effort! Not by trying! Not by practice! Not by setting our will-power against sin! But by trusting that God by His grace can do it. The only person who can "put away" sin, is the one who, having received Christ as Saviour, knows that Christ has "put away" his sin.

First, we must "lay aside." Peter summons us to abandon some ugly things—wickedness, guile, hypocrisy, envies, evil speaking. (2:1) From the root of wickedness all these noxious weeds spring. These must go from our hearts if we would grow. Weeds always choke out the plant, if we allow them to spread. All that challenges the supremacy of the Lord Jesus Christ must go, whether it be our sin or our righteousness. Sometimes even good things keep us from God's best. *Seek ye first the kingdom of God, and his righteousness; and all these things shall be added unto you* (Matthew 6:33). We must be careful of this. The choices you must make are not always between bad and good, right and wrong, but between the good and the best. *As for God, his way is perfect* (Psalm 18:30).

One of the great works of Christ is the cleaning up of our lives. We are told that as Christians we should lay *aside all malice, and all guile, and hypocrisies, and envies, and all evil speakings.* (I Peter 2:1) Our lives are to be clean inside and out. We are cleansed from sin within; we are to be cleansed from these evil fruits of sin. In order for us to be good witnesses of our Christianity there can be no difference between what we claim to believe and the way in which we act. Our behavior should be as orthodox as our belief. The words are still true: "What you are speaks so loudly that I cannot hear what you say." Let us live our Christianity in everything that we do. Let Christ live in us.

"Word" in 2:2 might be spelled with a capital "W," meaning Christ as well as His Word, for in the third verse we read that if you have once tasted of the Lord you will find He is gracious. He is the nourishment of our souls.

Peter says that when we become *children of God* (John 1:12) we are like newborn babies. (1:23) We need food to make us grow. This is just what God has provided in His Word. Desire the Word as newborn babes, and eating it, grow thereby. You will find that it tastes good. Christ will become real and gracious to you. (I Peter 1:23; 2:2,3) You can never grow as a Christian without food. Feed on the milk of His Word daily. Cultivate a desire for it!

Right here Peter turned to another figure and called Christ a "stone," rejected by men, but *precious in God's sight* (2:4). Everyone in this world has to do something with this "Stone," Christ Jesus. He is in every man's path. We can lift Him up and put Him in as the chief Cornerstone of our lives, which is God's will. But if we do not, we must stumble headlong over Him, tragically, to our death. To the Jews He was a stumbling-block and a rock of offense. To many today He is just that. What have you done with this precious "Cornerstone?" Is He in His rightful place in your life?

Dr. Robert Speer asked a young man one day after a conference, if he knew what I Peter 2:5 meant. He did not. Do you? *Ye also, as lively* [living] *stones, are built up a spiritual house*. This was the great man's answer. Some time ago they were tearing down an old wall over in that Eastern country, and as the stones fell away a human skeleton was exposed. This man had apparently been built up into the wall when alive. Investigation disclosed that this had been a common practice, and no doubt known to Peter and his audience. The living soul built into the wall was supposed to make it invulnerable and everlasting. Today, we put power into wires and run them through the walls of our buildings. Christians should be power-lines, life-lines, in the walls of their churches. Christ's life is the strength of the church and "ye also, as living stones, built up a spiritual house." (See Eph. 2:21.) Be a "live-wire" for Christ in your church!

We are not only "living stones" in a spiritual temple but each of us is a priest in this temple. Priests represent God to men, and men to God. Christians are a "holy priesthood." (2:5) Are you representing God to men by your life, and men to God by your intercessory prayer? As priests we do not offer lambs and goats today, but Paul tells us to offer ourselves a living sacrifice. (Romans 12:1)

DUTIES OF THE CHRISTIAN (Read I Peter 2:11—4:11)

Peter offers a simple program. Anyone can follow it. Any earnest seeker can find the way that Peter commands. His first suggestion is that we remember that we are "pilgrims." We are not settled here, but we are on our way to an eternal city. It is important that we keep this in mind, otherwise we will be tying our lives to stakes that will be shaken loose some day.

But with the Christian who has followed Peter's plan, all is different. He has invested time and thought and money in the pursuit of Christ's plan for his life. He finds life "sweeter as the years go by," and the end is the best of all!

The greatest satisfaction that can come to a Christian is to realize that he is pleasing His Lord and Saviour. In the power of the Lord, live for Christ in all phases of your life. Do not shut Him out of even the most insignificant parts. It will not be easy; the Devil will see to that. He will use every weapon against you. But Christ has won the victory over him and that victory may be yours for the asking.

Christians are not at home in this world. They are away from home, *as sojourners and pilgrims* (I Peter 2:11), for our "citizenship is in heaven." (Phil. 3:20) We are in the world, but, as Christians, we are not of it. (John 17:11,14)

We are to influence others by what we say and do. *Having your behaviour seemly among the Gentiles* (2:12). People are not reading much religious literature on paper, but they are doing a lot of reading in religious (or anti-religious) works by those professing Christ. It seems trite to say, but it is true that more are won to Christ by the true Christian life of the believer, than by any other means. If it is true that what you are speaks so loudly I cannot hear what you say, then it is equally true that your deeds speak so loudly that I cannot help but believe what you say. A Christian life must claim attention to itself by its very difference from the world-governed life around it.

Today some of you are subjected to severe tests. There are many things your companions do, both in business and recreation, that you cannot do as a Christian. Your action will be misunderstood and misrepresented. You will be called "narrow" and a "killjoy" or a "wet blanket." The best way to meet all such criticisms is not to assume an air of superiority or "holier than thou" attitude. Don't regard yourself as a martyr but accept the position with a smile and try to be helpful to those who are finding fault with you Nothing cools opposition like a gentle laugh of love. "Bless them that curse you, do good to them who despitefully use you," are Christ's words.

SQUARING YOUR LIFE

Put one of these in each of the corners of your life.

Honor all men!
  Try it and behold, men will honor you.

Love the brotherhood.
  Every social problem would be solved.

Fear God.
  The fear of the Lord is the beginning of wisdom.

Honor the King.
  Whether you voted for him or not. (I Peter 2:17)

As free, and not using your liberty for a cloak of maliciousness. (2:16) There is an amusing story of the early days of the Russian Revolution. After the Czar had abdicated, a stout old woman was seen walking leisurely down the middle of one of the busiest streets in St. Petersburg, at no small peril to herself and to the great confusion of traffic. A policeman pointed out to her that there was a walk for pedestrians, and that the street was for wagons, automobiles and horsemen. But she was not to be convinced. "I am going to walk just where I like," she said. "We've got liberty now." When we assert to "do as we like," we are as thoughtless and foolish as the old woman. Freedom is not a question of doing as we like. It is rather a question of doing as we ought. Do not let your liberty become license. The Christian is free from all that he may be the servant of all.

Behind a desk in a convention hall was a sign inviting everyone to refer any difficulties to Mr. Smith, and clearly displayed beneath these directions were the words, "Blessed is the man who can take the blame." Are you that kind? Can you patiently take blame you do not deserve? Can you smile cheerfully when somebody pitches into you for failure, when you did your level best? It is easy enough to feel that we deserve blame when we have consciously done wrong. Can we say, in the light of this lesson, that we understand Christian living when we are not willing to suffer for well-doing? We shall not have much to say about our undeserved suffering when we think of our Saviour. Our healing came by "His bruise." (Isaiah 53)

Patience in undeserved punishment is one way of testifying for Christ. A wicked crowd in his regiment took a violent dislike to one Christian soldier because he wouldn't swear or gamble or travel a loose life with them. His days were made miserable. But he never lost his temper nor gave in nor tried to pay them back, and in the end he led one of the worst of the fellows to Christ.

Christ lived the kind of life described in this letter of Peter's. And *he that saith he abideth in him ought himself also so to walk, even as he walked* (I John 2:6). The secret of walking *in newness of life* (Romans 6:4) is to *remember Jesus Christ* (II Tim. 2:8), and to rest in His strength.

THE CHRISTIAN

A babe (2:2), desiring the milk of the Word.
Living stone (2:5), built into the temple of life.
Priest—offering spiritual sacrifices.
Stranger—to keep himself unspotted from the world.
Pilgrim—do good deeds by the way.
Citizen—render obedience to rulers.
Man—honor all men, in the fear of God.
Servant—subject unto Christ.
Sufferer—to be patient, committing all to Christ.
Steward (4:10)
Oracles (4:11)

Christ also suffered for us (2:21). A lady was visiting in a hospital. She went up to a bed on which lay a wounded soldier, and said gently, "Thank you for being wounded for me." The young man's face brightened. That was a new thought to him. It made the pain more bearable to look upon it in that light. Do you realize that many years ago One was wounded for you? And that "One" was the Son of God Himself? Yes, He was wounded for my transgressions, by His stripes I am healed. (2:24)

We find in chapters 2 and 3 some instructions for the various relationships of our lives. First, there are some personal instructions. (2:1-12) Next we find our social relationships. Servants should obey their masters with respect, not only those who are good and considerate, but also those who are arbitrary. In 3:1-7 our home relationships are mentioned. Naturally the home begins with the marriage relationship. *Wives, be in subjection to your own husbands.* This means unselfish devotion, so as to win his love and admiration. This might sound unreasonable if we did not hear the injunction to husbands (3:7) that they *dwell with their wives according to knowledge.* This makes a wife subject to love which acts in knowledge and not according to selfish desires. It is manly for one to be tender toward his wife.

God's plan is that the love of husband and wife should be a mutual thing. Each one shall consider the other. The result of all this will be a marriage relationship in which prayers are not hindered. (3:7) Prayer is the surest secret of success in any married life. Nothing extinguishes the flame of prayer like friction in a home.

Peter gives the way to be happy in a world that is wretched. *For he that will love life, and see good days, let him refrain his tongue from evil, and his lips that they speak no guile: let him eschew evil, and do good; let him seek peace, and ensue it. For the eyes of the Lord are over the righteous, and his ears are open unto their prayers: but the face of the Lord is against them that do evil* (3:10-12). He quotes Psalm 34:12-14. This is a remedy that works today as well as it worked in David's time. The best way of making this life happy and prosperous is to keep from speaking evil and from slander and to be always ready to overcome evil with good.

Another important command is given in 3:15. This is for every one of us. *Be ready always to give an answer to every man that asketh you a reason of the hope that is in you.* Have you an intelligent answer to give to others of your trust in Christ? If not, stop right here and get one ready. What does Christ mean to you?

Be careful not to follow the world, *the will of the Gentiles* (4:3). The desire of the world is to get the Christian to do what they do.

A successful competitor in some college sports won a loving cup and on accepting it said, "Gentlemen, I have won this cup by the use of my legs. I trust I may never lose the use of my legs by the use of this cup."

Physiologists say a man's body contains chemicals whose total value is $1.50. And the gross total isn't raised any when he adds chemicals valued at, say, $25.00 a quart!

TRIALS OF THE CHRISTIAN (Read I Peter 4:12–5:14)

Nero was subjecting the Church to awful persecutions. Trials resulting from loyalty to Christ are inevitable. Christ sits as a refiner before the fire. It is with the most precious metals that the assayer takes the most pains, as he subjects them to the heat. Such fires melt the metal, and only the molten mass releases the alloy or takes its new form in the mold. Christ allows us to be subjected to the heat until all the dross is burned out and as the assayer sees his face in the molten mass and knows it is pure, so Christ can see His own face reflected in our life. The fires are always watched by our Saviour Himself. He never leaves the crucible. He will let nothing harm His own.

Don't be surprised when you are tried in the fire, as if some strange things were happening to you. (See 4:12.) Don't think that Christ has promised that we, as Christians, shall be spared from pain, or misfortunes, or death. In fact Christ says, *In this world ye shall suffer persecution*. This means no doubt that men will persecute the real Christian, because the world hates Christ and anything called by His name.

Peter exhorts the leaders of the Church to care for the flock. He tells them not *to lord it over them*, (5:3), but to serve them. Jesus had told Peter to *feed my sheep* (John 21). Under-shepherds are to receive their directions and rewards from the Chief Shepherd when He shall appear. (5:5) His crown of glory shall be fadeless.

The Christian life is like a jungle battle. Peter tells us who our enemy is. He is the Devil. His work is opposed to all that is good in this world. He is pictured as a roaring lion, seeking his prey. (5:8) This adversary is cagey, appearing sometimes as an angel of light, at another time as a serpent, coiled for the strike. He is always *seeking whom he may devour*. He is watching for the vulnerable spot, for the unguarded door to our hearts. Paul tells us what armor we should wear in Ephesians 6. But we need not be afraid, for *the God of all grace, who hath called us unto his eternal glory by Christ Jesus, after that ye have suffered a while, make you perfect, stablish, strengthen, settle you* (5:10).

"BOOK at a GLANCE"
I Peter

Privilege (1:1–2:10)

Name three privileges that a Christian has:

(1)...................... (2)...................... (3)......................

What two "precious" things are mentioned in chapter 1? ....

....

Duties (2:11–4:11)

What is the "precious" thing mentioned in chapter 2?

....

To what two things is a Christian likened in chapter 2? What verse tells us to be careful of our influence?

2: ....

Trials (4:12–5:14)

Why should we rejoice under sufferings?......................

....

What names are given to our worst enemy? (Chapter 5)

....

Minimum Daily Requirements / Spiritual Vitamins

Sunday: PRECIOUS FAITH I Peter 1:1-12

Monday: PRECIOUS BLOOD I Peter 1:13-25

Tuesday: PRECIOUS CORNERSTONE I Peter 2:1-10

Wednesday: PRECIOUS SAVIOUR I Peter 2:11-25

Thursday: PRECIOUS IS A MEEK AND QUIET SPIRIT
          I Peter 3:1-22

Friday: PRECIOUS SUFFERING OF CHRIST I Peter 4:1-19

Saturday: PRECIOUS CROWNS I Peter 5:1-14

Chapter 23

LET'S LOOK AT II PETER

II PETER PORTRAYS JESUS CHRIST,
OUR STRENGTH

CHRISTIAN VIRTUES (Read II Peter 1:1-21)

Do the days seem dark to you and does sin seem to abound everywhere? That is the way the world looked to the young Christians of Peter's day. So that they would not be discouraged by this outlook he showed them how to escape *the corruption that is in the world through lust* (1:4). Here it is, God has *given unto us all things that pertain unto life and godliness* (1:3).

Look at a poor man condemned to be hanged. Suppose a messenger comes to him and says: "The governor has taken your case into consideration, and I have brought you a purse of a thousand dollars." The poor man will say, "What good will it do me? I am to be hanged tomorrow." "Well, I have another message. He has considered your case and sent you the deed to a million dollar estate." The condemned man despairingly shakes his head and says, "What can I do with that? I must be hanged tomorrow." But the messenger goes on. "Stop! I have another offer to make. I have brought you the governor's own inauguration robe for you to wear with special favor." The condemned man burst into tears, as he says, "Do you intend to mock me? How would I appear ascending the steps of the gallows, wearing the governor's own robe?" Then the messenger says, "Wait, I have one more message. The governor has sent you a pardon. What do you say to that?" The poor man looks at him and says he doesn't believe it. But the messenger hands him the pardon, signed by the governor, with the official stamp upon it. Then the man leaps for joy, while tears of gratitude run down his face. Then the messenger says, "I am not through yet. I have brought you the pardon, the purse of gold, the deed, and the royal robe which are yours in addition." These are "all things" God has given us in Christ. His Son. With these nothing can defeat the young Christian.

The great evangelist, Moody, once said that men often fail because they try to do too large a business with too small a capital. So with Christians. But God has grace enough and capital enough. What would you think of a man who had a million dollars in the bank and drew out a penny a day? Remember, God's promises are exceedingly great and precious.

Do others know that you are a Christian by the way you look and act? You remember that night by the fire, when a smart young girl recalled that Peter had been with Jesus, Peter gave her some of the choice language of the Galilee fishing trade to prove he was not that kind. The crowd picked him out by his accent. (Mark

14:66-71) He gave himself away by a word. Later, the ruler picked him out as a companion of Jesus by his appearance and talk. The world recognizes us in exactly the same way. There is something about a person's whole bearing that proclaims him as a companion of Jesus Christ. As soon as we hear a man speak about Christ, we can tell what he is. He may stammer and stutter and make mistakes of grammar, but you know he is a Christian.

THE BIBLE'S MATH CHAPTER

Multiplication—"Grace and peace be multiplied" (1:2)
Addition—"Add to your faith" (1:5)
Subtraction—"Purged from his sins" (1:9)

There are seven steps going up from faith, and the last one is love. These steps are the Christian virtues that every Christian should have. Let's climb slowly and thoughtfully up this flight of stairs, and see how far we have gone. Add to your faith virtue, knowledge, self-control, patience, godliness, brotherly kindness, love. (1:5-7)

The fuller the measure of these virtues, the greater will be our knowledge of Jesus Christ our Lord. Know Christ, for to know Him is life eternal, and in none other is there salvation. (See Acts 4:12.) A man recently gave directions to another who stopped to ask him the way to a certain street. "That's the best way, is it?" asked the inquirer, a little doubtfully. "It is the only way," was the quick response. "The other road will land you back where you started." It is only in Christ that we find progress. He is the Way to Heaven and Life.

Someone has said this is a seven-story-and-basement building. Add story to story, but be sure to put faith at the foundation. If you try to build without the proper base the building will become top-heavy. To be sure, faith is the foundation grace. But a foundation is of little use if no building follows. During the days of the depression it was a common sight to see the framework of a great building standing stark and gaunt, with weeds growing around it, abandoned by the men who had begun a good work but for some reason ceased before it was finished. The foundation was substantial and adequate, but for years was entirely useless because nothing was added.

Peter, like Paul, warns Christians from standing still. Don't remain babes in Christ, being tripped over by every new teaching, but grow strong in the Lord.

But he that lacketh these things is blind, and cannot see afar off (1:9). Near-sighted Christians we will be, "unfit" for enlistment in God's army, if we do not have these virtues. Be sure of your position in Christ. Don't ever doubt your calling in Him. Spare no effort to put God's call and choice beyond all doubt. Spare no effort in prayer, in study and in talking with Christians.

A Christian's ambition should be to have a full life. Peter wants you to have an abundant entrance into the Haven of Rest, Christ's eternal kingdom. (1:11) Enter in with sails unfurled, bearing a precious cargo of passengers and loaded with "good works" that your reward may be great to the glory of God.

Peter, like Paul, was conscious of his approaching death. He has a beautiful name for death, *the putting off of my tabernacle* (1:14). Moffatt says, "The folding up of my tent." Because he knew he was about to leave them, he wanted to stir them up by putting them in remembrance of what he so well knew. His memory pictured before him the great transfiguration scene. There he had witnessed the glory of Christ. Any doubt as to His reality or of His coming again in power was forever banished from his mind. God Himself had borne testimony of His glory and honor, and a Voice said, *This is my beloved Son, in whom I am well pleased*. He heard the Voice from above. This is the testimony of Deity. Now Peter knew. He was sure. He wanted them to know that he was not telling them fairy stories when he told them of the power and coming of the Lord Jesus Christ, but he was an eye-witness of His majesty. He says, "I was there. It is true."

CHRISTLESS TEACHERS (Read II Peter 2:1-22)

Are the times in which we live hard, and temptations strong, and opposition powerful? Expect it and rise above it. We are warned that it shall be so. The world always has been and always will be full of antagonism to the truth, and to those who speak it. But God will bring it to naught. In the meantime, *The Lord knoweth how to deliver the godly out of temptations* (2:9). Let us be strong and steady.

Peter tells of the coming, the influence, and the doom of the false teachers, in this dark and appalling chapter. We need not be surprised at their coming, for Christ warned us of that in Matt. 7:15; 24:11,24, and we have listened to Paul's words about them to Timothy (I Tim. 4:1-3; II Tim. 3:1-9).

What a black list is this account which Peter gives us of their deeds. There is no softening of the shade from one end to the other. It is a black picture indeed. Read it! No wonder Peter warned the Church of false prophets!

1. False Propaganda

But there were false prophets also among the people, even as there shall be false teachers among you, who privily shall bring in damnable heresies, even denying the Lord that bought them and bring upon themselves swift destruction. And many shall follow their pernicious ways; by reason of whom the way of truth shall be evil spoken of. And through covetousness shall they with feigned words make merchandise of you: whose judg-

ment now of a long time lingereth not, and their damnation slumbereth not (II Pet. 2:1-3).

The false teachers of today do just what is told here. First, they *privily bring in damnable heresies*. They do it subtly. They don't believe in the deity of Christ—that Jesus, who was born of a virgin, was very God. If they said this, people would hesitate to follow them. Peter describes the "damnable heresy" they bring in. This is it—"denying the Lord that bought them." It does not say that they deny the Lord that taught them. Practically every false religion acknowledges Christ as a great teacher, but they will not accept Him as Saviour, the One who "bought" us with His own precious blood. They deny the blood atonement.

2. Blood Test

This is the mark by which to test and reject the false teacher. Ask for credentials of teachers who are abroad today. When any teacher does not put the cross at the center of his teaching, beware! Turn from him. Our redemption is in the blood. Jesus bought us with His blood.

3. Popularity Test

These teachers are popular. *Many shall follow their pernicious ways* (2:2). Don't think it strange that Christian Science, Theosophy, Unity, and a score of others can procure a large following. Peter told us they would. Men do not want to be told that they need a Saviour. That makes them admit that they are sinners. They only want to be taught, not "bought." *The way of truth shall be evil spoken of* (2:2). All of these false teachings talk about "truth" but they forget that Christ said, *I am the way, the truth, and the life: no man cometh unto the Father, but by me* (John 14:6). He is not just a part of truth—He IS truth. He is not a "wayshower"—He is THE WAY. He does not come to show us how to live. He is LIFE. It is easy to distort truth.

4. Vocabulary Test

With feigned words make merchandise of you (2:3). Words mean so little in many of these false religions. There is a new meaning given to so many words. They say they believe in everything but when we ask them what they mean, it is far from what the Scripture says. They keep the form of words, but the meaning is pumped out. It is like an Easter egg. We put holes in either end and then blow out all the inside. The form of the egg is there, but the real meat is gone. Christ said that men would even say, *Lord, Lord,* but He would say, *Depart from me; I never knew you.* Words mean nothing unless there is heart in their meaning.

5. Punishment!

There is only one thing God can do with this kind of men, and that is to destroy them. *Light that is trifled with becomes lightning.* Peter declares with no uncertain sound that that shall be the end of false teachers who cover themselves with the cloak of the Church. (2:3-9) They shall certainly be punished. God did not even spare the angels who sinned! He sent a flood upon a godless world in Noah's day. Sodom and Gomorrah were reduced to ashes. All of these were as a warning to the godless of every generation of what God has in store for him. One thing we can be sure of, no matter how severe the judgment for the false teacher may be, the deliverance of God's people is promised. *The Lord knoweth how to deliver.* Leave the punishment of the wicked with God.

CHRIST'S COMING (Read II Peter 3:1-18)

False teaching about Christ, which denies His Deity and power, issues in false thinking. The first question it raises is about the coming of Christ. To help the Church in this, Peter reminds them of the things Jesus had said. Men misunderstood Him and thought His return might be in that generation. Peter tells them that time is nothing with God—*a thousand years with Him is but a day*. He will keep this promise as He has kept all of His promises, but according to His own time.

The Lord is not slack concerning his promise, [he is not] *willing that any should perish, but that all should come to repentance* (3:9). The last days are to be sad days, for scoffers shall make fun, and say, "Ha ha, where is the promise of Christ's coming? As far as we can see, everything is going on just as it has from the beginning. Nature goes along in the even tenor of her way. There have been no signs of any radical change. The promise of His coming has failed." These scoffers were evil men, but the sad truth today is that good men scoff at the promise of His coming. They make sport of the great hope of the Church. How illogical was their reasoning about Christ's not coming. Here they are! He had not yet come, hence He was not coming. Nothing different had happened, hence nothing unusual was going to happen. Because our Lord has not come as yet, shall we give up hope? No, indeed. Rather, rejoice in the fact that His coming draws nearer every day.

Peter reminds these skeptics that a mighty flood did drown the world once, and Christ likened His coming to the flood in Matthew 24:37, 38. No doubt Peter heard Him say it. But next time God will destroy the earth by fire. Will it be literal fire? Was the flood literal? Stored within the earth are oils and gases and fire enough to burn it up. Volcanoes are the release of these elements. Scientists tell us we are sitting on a crust of earth only thirty miles in depth. Beneath this is a mass of molten matter. At a word, God could release a spout which would bury the earth in literal fire, or our earth may collide with some other heavenly body.

We know that, when God's clock strikes the hour, the earth will melt with a fervent heat. The earth shall be burned up and in the great explosion the heavens will pass away. Then *new heavens and a new earth* will emerge (3:13). We are living today in the age of atomic and hydrogen bombs. Their description can almost be found in these verses written nearly 2000 years ago.

What effect should all this have on our lives? Peter answers in verse 14. We will be diligent in our service, striving always to be peaceable, spotless and blameless in character. Don't grow careless because He is delaying, for one day the Lord will come suddenly. Be patient while He delays, knowing that He does it because He is long-suffering and would give the last man, woman and child a chance to accept Him.

What lives we ought to live while we wait for His coming! We may hasten it by our holy living. Faith in the return of our Lord must lead to this. Then we may hasten it by a holy conversation. Watch your speech. Don't forget to look forward with an eager gaze. Then be diligent that you be "found of Him." (3:14) Are you looking forward to His coming? What effect has this hope upon your life and conversation?

Peter's last word of warning is "Beware!" This is a note of caution. *Beware lest ye also are influenced by these skeptics and fall away from your steadfast faith.*

The remedy against falling back is to "grow"—make progress. *Grow in grace and in the knowledge of our Lord and Saviour Jesus Christ.* Are you growing in your knowledge? Christian knowledge is an effective weapon against heresy. Christianity without a creed cannot stand against the attacks of the critics. A growing Christian becomes conscious of his sin. In a room full of loathsome things, if one ray of light is admitted, we will see some, but when more light comes in we see more of the horrors. So the more we allow Christ to come into our hearts, the more of our sinfulness we will see. Then when we have dealt with the sin in our lives, we can begin to do something to make progress. Pray much. Be dependent on the Holy Spirit. Sit at Jesus' feet and learn of Him through His holy Word, and give yourself unreservedly to Him.

"BOOK at a GLANCE"
II Peter

Christian Virtues (1:1-21)

What virtues shall we add to our faith to produce a strong Christian life?..

How can we become partakers of the divine nature?......

....

What name does Peter give to death?................................

....

What experience made Peter so sure of his faith?..........

....

Christian Teachers (2:1-22)

What is the "damnable heresy" that false teachers will bring in? ....

What Scripture proves that popularity is not a safe test for religious teachers?..

Give three examples that prove God does not spare sinners. ....

Christ's Coming (3:1-18)

What is man's attitude about Christ's second coming?

....

How shall the earth finally be destroyed?........................

....

What should be our attitude as we wait for Christ's coming? ....

What do you discover about the new world?..................

....

....

Minimum Daily Requirements / Spiritual Vitamins

Sunday: CHRISTIAN VIRTUES II Peter 1:1-14

Monday: CHRIST'S WORD EXALTED II Peter 1:15-21

Tuesday: CHRISTLESS TEACHERS II Peter 2:1-14

Wednesday: CHRIST AGAINST THE BACKSLIDER II Peter 2:15-22

Thursday: CHRIST'S COMING SCOFFED II Peter 3:1-9

Friday: CHRIST'S COMING ASSURED II Peter 3:10-18

Saturday: CHRIST OUR HOPE II Peter 1:1–3:18

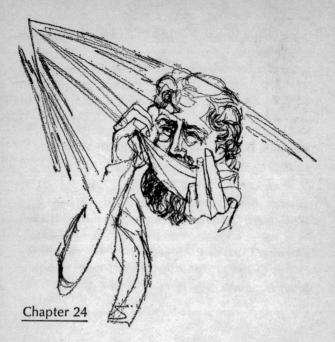

Chapter 24

LET'S LOOK AT I, II, III JOHN and JUDE

JESUS CHRIST: OUR LIFE;
THE TRUTH; THE WAY; OUR KEEPER

RIGHT BEHAVIOR (Read I John 1:1–3:24)

John gives us seven tests of Christian behavior. Read these and find what your "rating" is as a Christian. They are easy to find because each of these tests is introduced by "if we say" or "he that saith." The test is this—"If we say" one thing, and do another, we are not living as Christ would want us to, in full fellowship with Himself. How much easier it is to talk than it is to do. As Moody said, "We talk cream and live skim milk."

TEST ONE—WALK IN THE LIGHT

If we say that we have fellowship with Him [the God of light] *and walk in darkness, we lie, and do not the truth* (1:6). Here is the first, "if we say." Have you underlined it?

Is there known sin in your life? If there is, you are not walking with Christ. His presence throws light on your conscience and heart and shows the presence of sin in the life. (Eph. 5:13) A Christian who is walking in fellowship with God will enjoy fellowship with other Christians. (I John 1:7) He will be found with them in Christian service. Sin separates us from God and from our fellow men. You remember when Adam and Eve sinned, that they hid themselves from God. You notice how even a child will run and hide when he has done something wrong. There is sin in our nature, and the light of God's presence will reveal it if we are walking with Him. Have you ever picked up a stone that has been lying on the ground for a long time? The minute you lift it, living things move in every direction to flee from the light. Light reveals sin. Known sin will keep you from fellowship with Christ, but fellowship with Christ will keep you from sin. Do you ask Him to throw His searchlight upon your heart?

It is wonderful to walk in the light and know just where you are going. Darkness makes men grope. When you enter a dark room you grope about, knocking your shins on a chair or stool and groaning when you do. You feel perturbed within, not knowing where you are going. Then you find the light switch and snap it on. Light floods the room! Now you can walk in and out among the chairs and tables and lamps, with no trouble at all. Light made all the difference.

The world, under Satan's dominion, is in darkness. Unbelievers are blinded and have not the light of Christ's presence shining on their path, but it is our privilege to walk in light.

SECOND TEST—ADMIT YOU ARE A SINNER

If we say that we have no sin, we deceive ourselves, and the truth is not in us (1:8). You cannot walk with God and practice sin in your life at the same time. But God takes care of the sin question. God keeps showing us the sin in our lives. On the cross He redeemed us from the penalty of sin once and for all. But let us know, too, that He keeps cleansing us from the sins that creep into our lives by our contact with this world. We must admit it and confess it. (1:8,9)

When a farmer plows his field, he throws out every stone that he finds. But the next year as the plow goes deep in the furrow, he finds other stones that had remained hidden the year before. He throws these aside as they turn up. Then the next year the same thing occurs. So in our lives! God will reveal by the plow of His Spirit the sins that are hidden in our lives, that we did not know were there. Don't be discouraged but use His remedy.

If we confess our sins, He is faithful and just to forgive us our sins, and to cleanse us from all unrighteousness (1:9). One day we will be freed from the very presence of sin in our bodies. That is when Jesus comes. Then our bodies *shall be changed, in a moment, in the twinkling of an eye.* Until that time our only perfection is in Him.

Confess your sin. Don't cry over it. Don't pray in an indefinite way. Name it before God. Is it pride, lack of trust, anger, love of pleasure more than God? Well, whatever it is, lay it out before God and tell Him what it is. Call it by name. Then claim God's promise. *He is faithful and just,* not only *to forgive us our sins* but *to cleanse us from all unrighteousness.* A human parent can forgive us our misbehavior, but only God can cleanse our lives from sin.

God has provided a sure victory over sin. In 2:1 we

read, "If any man sin, we have an advocate." There is no allowance for sin, but God has made ample provision in case we do sin. We should not sin; there should never be a compromise with evil, but there is a provision in case we do. On every ship we find an ample supply of life belts. It is not that the boat intends to sink, but they are put there in case of shipwreck. So, *if any man sin, we have an advocate*. It is God's provision in case of need. Thank Him that He has cleansed you and step out, knowing this fact. Don't wait for feeling; accept His promise.

You see, no one can be walking in the light of His presence and be ignorant of the fact that he is sinning. *If we say that we have not sinned, we make Him a liar, and His word is not in us* (1:10).

Admit sin 1:8-10
Confess it to God and to
    those you have wronged....................................1:9
Victory—because you have an Advocate...........2:1

THIRD TEST—OBEY GOD'S WILL

He that saith, I know Him, and keepeth not His commandments, is a liar, and the truth is not in him (2:4). Obedience is a real test. God makes a very strong statement. If you say you are a Christian and do not obey Him, you are a liar. The man that is a Christian keeps God's commandments. *Hereby we do know that we know Him, if we keep His commandments* (2:3).

What are Christ's commandments? Love the Lord thy God with all thy heart, soul and mind, and thy neighbor as thyself. Do you love God that way? Put yourself to a few tests. Do you spend more time listening to the radio than you do to God? Then you don't love Him with all your heart. Are you ambitious to carry out some plan in your life that you hope will bring you fame or wealth or just enjoyment? Don't say you know God when you won't keep His commandments. Do you know His will for your life? Do you want to? This is a test of your Christian life. Are you obedient to His Word? To His still small voice? Many times we do not want to let God talk to us. We will not listen to Him because we are afraid of His will for us. Youth looks for a career. God has a career for each one of us. He has a plan for every step of our lives, for *the steps of a good man are ordered of the Lord.* We must obey in everything for *whatsoever is not of faith is sin.*

You will begin to know what God wishes as you grow to know Him better. A group of fellows were going to a nightclub of bad reputation. They stopped to ask a young chap to go along. "I can't go," he said. "Why not?" his associates asked. "Well, because my mother wouldn't want me to." "How do you know she wouldn't? She doesn't even know we are going." "Because I know my mother," was his very wise reply. This is true when you learn to know God—you will know what His desires are. (3:24)

Read Christ's Word. Know what it says for you! Live it!

FOURTH TEST—IMITATE CHRIST

He that saith he abideth in Him ought himself also so to walk, even as He walked. (2:6)

We should be Christlike in all our life. Christ says, *Ye are the salt of the earth.* Salt preserves food from spoiling. Are you the preservative of your crowds? Do you keep the language clean? Do you refrain from using God's name in vain? Does your presence keep them from doing questionable things?

A little Chinese girl said, "I know why Christ said, *Ye are the salt of the earth.* Because salt makes folks thirsty and Christians should make others thirsty for Christ." Are you making folks thirsty?

A Christian is "I" following Christ—"CHRIST-I-AN." Have you a golden text for your life? A good question to ask is, "What would Jesus do?"

Few people really try to find Christ. So Christ wants others to see Him reflected in us. In the famous Sistine Chapel in Rome, the beauty of the art is in the ceiling. As you enter you are given a mirror. It seems strange to see people walking around looking down when the paintings are above. But they see all the glory reflected in the mirrors before them, without breaking their necks. Be a reflector. Let the beauty of Jesus be seen in you.

FIFTH TEST—LOVE OTHERS

He that saith he is in the light, and hateth his brother, is in darkness even until now (2:9).

Another acid test of the Christian life is love. (2:7-11) Love absolutely changes a person. Someone has said of a man in love, "You can tell a man in love, but can't tell him much." Love makes us have a concern for the welfare of others.

God speaks of love to others, personal attitudes. There are three chief attitudes towards others: hatred, which is murder (3:15); indifference—a feeling akin to hate—no concern (4:20,21); love—love shows itself in different ways (2:9-11; 3:14); physically—concern for welfare (3:16-18); spiritually—concern for another's soul. We should want to love as God loves. We should be as concerned as He for the souls of men.

SIXTH TEST—RELATIONSHIP TO THE WORLD

If any man love the world, the love of the Father is not in him (2:12-17).

We live in a present evil age. (Gal. 1:4) The scheme

of things as they exist today is not the standard for the Christian. Whenever you find him obeying them, he is walking on forbidden ground.

All sins may be put under three categories: 1. Lust of the flesh; 2. Lust of the eye; 3. Pride of life.

If you follow Jesus' temptation in Luke 4:1-13, you will see that each of these three approaches was used by the Devil.

Temptations come through the body and its appetites and passions. The Devil tempted Jesus in this way first. Jesus had been fasting forty days, and every atom of His being cried for bread. How plausible was Satan's temptation! It was the same appeal to appetite that Satan made to Eve. In all these thousands of years the Devil had invented no new weapon of attack. *Command that these stones become bread*. The temptation for self-gratification is one of the strongest that can assail us. Appetite is still one of the most vulnerable points, when Satan attacks us.

If thou therefore wilt worship me, all shall be thine (Luke 4:7). Satan was working his second trick. How men worship at the altar of riches and honor, because they long for what their eyes see of this world. Your eyes can blacken your soul! Be careful what you see. If you throw a white tennis ball against a sooty wall, there will be a black mark left upon it. If your eye is thrown against impure objects, you can be sure a mark will be left upon your mind and heart. Be careful what you see!

Everyone wants spectacular success. The Devil took Jesus to the pinnacle of the temple and told Him to cast Himself down and if He was the Son of God, He would be kept by angels. It was a proposal to leap from the pinnacle of the temple into immediate popularity. It is a temptation for anyone to desire popularity. We all have human ambitions. How many men of genius have been led astray because the glittering prize of ambition has been held before them! We want to win it at a single stroke. How strong is the temptation to take a short cut to our ambition whether of education or wealth or position and power. We are in danger of selling our very souls to gain our end! Jesus was offered the world for a word. Who would refuse to pay this price?

SEVENTH TEST—PROVE CHRIST IS RIGHTEOUS BY YOUR LIFE

Who is a liar but he that denieth [by life] *that Jesus is the Christ?* (2:22) Do we acknowledge Christ by our life and lips? *If ye know that He is righteous, ye know that every one that doeth righteousness is born of Him* (2:29). Others watch us to see if we "do righteousness." He who abides in Christ will bear the same fruit in his life that Christ bears and that is righteousness. We must not deny Christ by our life. Let us be Christlike in all that we do. (3:1-10)

Whosoever is born of God doth not commit [practice] *sin.* It is possible for a Christian under strong temptation, to fall into sin for the time, but he will not keep practicing it. If a person continually practices sin, he may well doubt his conversion! We should consider sin as God does. He gave a Saviour to redeem us from sin. Sin cost God His Son!

RIGHT BELIEF (Read I John 4:1–5:11)

We need a creed by which to live. The word "creed" comes from the Latin word, "credo"—"I believe." There are sins of the body which we all commit, but there are sins of the heart and dispositions as well. God is as interested in what you believe as in how you act.

Your sin can start in your intellect. What do you believe? Christ wants to be our only Teacher. What we believe determines how we act.

Is a creed necessary? Read John 3:16 and see if you think it is. It says, *Whosoever believeth hath everlasting life.* Christianity is Christ-centered. Christ out of Christianity leaves nothing. This means death. If we believe not, we shall die, but if we believe we shall live. (Rom. (10:9,10)

Many Christians are spiritual babes in Christ. They catch a cold with every new "wind of doctrine." They are susceptible to all about them. When doubt fills their minds, they sink in despair. Hence everyone ought to be given a way whereby he can test every religion to see if it be true. Especially is this true in this day of so many religious beliefs.

John states the test very clearly in 4:1-3. *Beloved, believe not every spirit, but try the spirits whether they are of God: because many false prophets are gone out into the world. Hereby know ye the Spirit of God; every spirit that confesseth that Jesus Christ is come in the flesh is of God: and every spirit that confesseth not that Jesus Christ is come in the flesh is not of God: and this is that spirit of antichrist.*

John makes some plain statements in these verses above.

1. That Jesus Christ is *come in the flesh*—"incarnos." (4:1,2; 5:20,21)

2. We must believe in the Deity of Christ. (4:15; 5:5) That He is the Son of God, the only-begotten Son.

3. We must believe that Christ is our Saviour. (5:10-12)

Love is the supreme test of our Christian faith. *We know that we have passed from death unto life, because we love the brethren. He that loveth not his brother abideth in death* (3:14). The word LOVE occurs 48 times in this first epistle of John. We find out how "love" acts in I Corinthians 13. Read it again and refresh your memory.

Love is like an irrigating dam. It is only what runs out that does any good. Love must flow out to every man; must build hospitals, send missionaries, feed the hungry, protect the weak—in short, be a modern Good Samaritan. That is what a real Christian will do with his salvation, not just talk about it, but live it, use it, send it out for a blessing.

He that loveth not knoweth not God; for God is love (4:8). Love is the first instinct of the renewed heart. Where do we get our love? From within? No, from above. *We love Him, because He first loved us* (4:19). What if we do not love? God describes us like this, *We know not God.*

We should show our love to Him by loving one another. (4:7) He who has love in his heart has fellowship with God. (4:16) But where there is no love, there is no fellowship. (4:19-21)

RICH REWARDS (Read I John 5:12-21)

The rewards of a life in Christ are stated in the last verses of chapter 5:12-21.

Assurance of eternal life 5:13
Power of prayer 5:14,15
Power of intercession 5:16
Victory . . . . 5:18 and 5:4,5

Underline the word "KNOW" in verses 12-20. We can have a confidence when we know Christ. John uses the word "know" over forty times in his epistles. True Christianity is more than a creed—it is something that can be known and felt. We know that Christ was manifested to take away our sins. We know that we have passed from death unto life. We know that whatsoever we ask we shall receive. Again and again John assures us of these truths.

What we KNOW

Find these references—2:3,4,13,14,20,21,29; 3:2,5,14, 15,19,24; 4:2,6,13,16; 5:2,12,15,18-20.

II John Portrays Jesus Christ, The Truth.
III John Portrays Jesus Christ, The Way.
Jude Portrays Jesus Christ, Our Keeper.

"BOOKS at a GLANCE"
I John

Right Behavior (1:1–3:24)

In what verses do you find the phrases "if we say" or "he that saith?"..

....

Give four out of seven tests of the Christian's behavior.

....

....

If we wish to experience forgiveness of sins, what must we do?..

....

Right Belief (4:1–5:11)

What must we believe about Christ?.................................

....

What is the supreme test of our Christian faith?.............

....

Rich Rewards (5:12-21)

Name the rich rewards of the Christian stated in 5:12-21. ....

....

....

II John

In II John, Jesus is portrayed as....................................

....

III John

In III John, Jesus is portrayed as...................................

....

Jude

In Jude, Jesus is portrayed as.......................................

....

256

Minimum Daily Requirements / Spiritual Vitamins

Sunday: WALKING IN FELLOWSHIP I John 1:1–2:14

Monday: WALKING AS CHILDREN OF GOD I John 2:15–3:24

Tuesday: WALKING IN LOVE I John 4:1-21

Wednesday: WALKING IN KNOWLEDGE I John 5:1-21

Thursday: WALKING IN TRUTH II John 1–13

Friday: WALKING IN THE WAY III John 1–14

Saturday: WALKING WITHOUT FALLING Jude 1–25

Chapter 25

LET'S LOOK AT REVELATION

REVELATION PORTRAYS JESUS CHRIST,
OUR TRIUMPHANT KING

Revelation is the only book of prophecy in the New Testament. It is the only book in the Divine library that especially promises a blessing to those who read and hear. "Blessed" is a strong word. *Blessed is he that readeth,* is what the book of Revelation says of itself, but after reading the first chapters about the churches, and the last chapters describing heaven, not many of us read much in this book.

Revelation presents a glorious reigning Christ. The Gospels presented Him as a Saviour, One who came to take the curse of sin, but this last book tells us about the reign of Christ on this earth which Satan wants to control. It tells of Christ's complete and eternal victory over Satan. It describes Satan's defeat and punishment, first for a thousand years, then eternally. It tells more about Satan's final doom than any other book. No wonder Satan doesn't want men to read it! In all sorts of ways he has prevented it. We hear people say, "Oh, I can't make head or tail of it." "It doesn't mean anything to me." "No one can understand it."

Does "revelation" mean a riddle? Most people seem to think it does, when speaking of this book. No, it means just the opposite—"unveiling." It is written in symbols. *It was sent and signified* by the angel to John. The deaf and dumb have a sign language. Each gesture is filled with meaning. So is every sign in Revelation. There are 300 symbols in this book, and each has a definite meaning. Symbols are wonderful and speak great truths. The American flag is a symbol. It is only red, white and blue bunting, but it represents the United States of America to us. The cross is a symbol, but it speaks of our salvation and God's love. So all the symbols in Revelation have a meaning.

Christ is the theme of this wonderful book. Let us see Him in and through it all. It gives an authentic portrait of the Lord Jesus as the Triumphant One. No less than twenty-six times do we find in it Christ's sacrificial title "Lamb." (5:6) In addition we see a vision of the future of the Church and the world in relation to Him.

Revelation is a wonderful way to finish the story which was begun in Genesis. All that was begun in the Book of Beginnings (Genesis) is consummated in Revelation. In Genesis the heaven and earth were created. In Revelation we see a new heaven and a new earth. In Genesis the sun and moon appear; in Revelation we read that they have no need of the sun or moon, for Christ is the light of the new heaven. In Genesis there is a garden; in Revelation there is a holy city. In Genesis there is the marriage of the first Adam; in Revelation the marriage supper of the second Adam, Jesus Christ. In Genesis we see the beginning of sin; in Revelation sin is done away. So we can follow the appearance of the great adversary, Satan, and sorrow and pain and tears in Genesis, and see their doom in Revelation.

God had determined from the beginning that His Son would be the Ruler of this universe. *For unto us a child is born, unto us a son is given: and the government shall be upon his shoulder: and his name shall be called Wonderful, Counsellor, The mighty God, The everlasting Father, The Prince of Peace. Of the increase of his government and peace there shall be no end, upon the throne of David, and upon his kingdom, to order it, and to establish it with judgment and with justice from henceforth even for ever. The zeal of the Lord of hosts will perform this* (Isa. 9:6,7). But we see another desiring the rule of this world—Satan. Man, also, has tried to establish himself and to build a civilization without God. The outcome of all this is found in the last book of the Bible.

Revelation is the greatest drama of all time. The plot is tense throughout; the final scene is glorious, for Christ comes into His own. The Hero is our Lord Himself; the villain is the Devil. The actors are the seven churches. The characters unloosed by the seals of chapters 6 and 7, are introduced by the "four horsemen." Then those summoned by the trumpets in turn leave the center of the scene of action, and we see the Antichrist, the world ruler, stalking across the stage. (Chap. 13). This incarnation of the Devil himself is determined to set up his own kingdom and be worshiped of men. But Christ brings all to naught. This majestic One, bringing His hosts with Him, comes forth—the long-looked-for King of kings and Lord of lords. He drives His enemies from the stage in utter defeat, and the drama is brought to a close. (chap.

19) In one titanic struggle He destroys what man has built up, and pronounces that the end of all things is at hand.

After all the struggle has ended, and the beasts have been destroyed and the Devil bound, and *the former things are passed away,* then we hear these words, full of hope, *Behold, I make all things new.* (Rev. 21:4,5) This book brings to a climax the great story commenced in Genesis, and as all good stories should end, it ends "And they lived happily ever after."

NOTICE THE 7'S IN THIS BOOK

- Seven Churches
- Seven seals
- Seven trumpets
- Seven signs
- Seven last plagues
- Seven dooms
- Seven new things

PAST—THE THINGS WHICH THOU HAST SEEN
(Read Revelation 1:1-18)

This first scene presents the Hero, the Lord Jesus Christ, the glorified One. Here is the last picture of Jesus Christ given in the New Testament. Many artists have tried to portray Him, but they have failed. Here is an authentic portrait. (1:13-16) He is standing in the midst of the seven golden lampstands, representing the churches. (v. 20) Lampstands prove that the Church is to be a light-bearer. *Ye are the light of the world.* Many churches today seem to exist more for entertainment, bazaars, and to promote money-making schemes, than to be lights to shine in a dark place!

Christ is likened to a "son of man," but it is clear from the vision that the One whom John saw was more than human. He was the Son of Man. Everything symbolizes majesty and judgment, and this thought of judgment strikes the keynote of the book. Christ is presented to the whole world as judge. Read the description of this wonderful One carefully. (1:12-18)

John's vision was not of this age in which we are living, but of a future day when men shall appear before Christ to be judged. (John 5:27-29) Now, we may have all of God's grace, mercy and forgiveness for the taking. Now, Christ is before us to be judged. We can reject Him if we choose. In Revelation, John is picturing Christ in judgment. The day of mercy is past, when we stand before the Judge of judges, the King of kings, the Lord of lords.

When John saw this glorious One, he fell at His feet as dead, so overpowering was the vision. (1:17) But Christ's words were reassuring. He said He was the living One, and though He had been dead, He was alive forevermore, and held the keys of death and Hades. Then follows the command to write what is found in this book. (1:19) We do not have the usual picture of Christ starting in Bethlehem and ending at the Mount of Olives, but here we have His life in heaven, as the crown and culmination of all.

Have you ever seen the Lord? When Moses saw Him his face shone. Job abhorred himself and repented in ashes. Isaiah saw himself unclean. Saul fell down and worshiped Him as Saviour. What would happen to us if we really saw the Lord?

The alarm goes off and wakens us out of a sound sleep. What is the first thought that strikes you? Does some worry seize you and tie you into a knot at once? That problem? That conference at eleven? The exam? Or do you think of Christ in your first waking moment—His love, His plan for you, His power over your trials of the day? Is He first as the day breaks upon you? Then when night comes, do you finish the day with fears of tomorrow or do you lie down to rest in the arms of the Lord, trusting Him completely? Is Jesus first and last to you?

PRESENT—THE THINGS WHICH ARE
(Read Revelation 1:20—3:22)

Suppose you should find in your morning mail a letter from Jesus! You would read that letter as you never read any letter before in your life. You would be very likely to do everything it said, wouldn't you? Well, in the second and third chapters of Revelation we have seen seven letters from Jesus to Christians, and these seven letters are to you and to me!

"If Christ Came to Chicago" was a book that made a great stir some years ago. "If Christ wrote a letter to your church" do you think it would make a stir in your church? What do you think He would be likely to write?

In the second and third chapters we find Christ's love letters to His churches.

These churches named were churches which actually existed in John's day. In dealing with them, He seems to give us a picture of all churches. In every age there have been these same characteristic qualities to be found.

Discover where you find Christ at the end of this Church Age. *Behold, I stand at the door, and knock: if any man hear my voice, and open the door, I will come in to him, and will sup with him, and he with me* (3:20). He is outside, knocking to get in. The church will not let Him in, but He pleads with the individual: *If any man . . . open the door, I will come in.* Have you opened your heart's door to Christ? Sing:

"Into my heart, into my heart,

Come into my heart, Lord Jesus;

Come in today, come in to stay,

Come into my heart, Lord Jesus."

FUTURE—THE THINGS WHICH SHALL BE HEREAFTER
(Read Revelation 4:1—22:21)

The scene shifts from earth to heaven.

First the throne of God comes into view. (4:1-3) Revelation becomes the "Book of the Throne." This is the great central fact which pervades the book. This throne speaks of judgment. The throne of grace is no longer seen. The scene is a court-room. The Judge of all the earth is on the bench; the twenty-four elders are the jury, representing the twelve patriarchs of the Old Testament and the twelve Apostles of the New. (4:4) The seven spirits of God (4:5; 5:6) are the prosecutor, and the four living creatures are court attendants, ready to carry out the will of the Judge.

For 1900 years God has been calling upon the earth to bow the knee to His Son, the Lord Jesus Christ, and they would not. They would not do it through the preaching of the Gospel of the love of God, so now judgment is necessary. John announces what he sees acted before his eyes. Acting as eyes and ears for us, much like an announcer at a great football game or political convention, he describes the moves and presents a clear picture.

The day of tribulation begins with the opening of the seven seals. (chap. 6) A swift preliminary glimpse of the course of events here below in judgment days is presented. This is the beginning of the end.

This describes the Great Tribulation period spoken of by the prophet Jeremiah in Jeremiah 30 as the *time of Israel's sorrow*. Christ also referred to it as a great tribulation, such as has never happened upon the earth. (Matt. 24:21) During the Great Tribulation God will allow sin to work out its tragic results. God's hand will be lifted from man and beast. The earth will be filled with war, hunger, famine and pestilence. We cannot paint too dark a picture of this terrible period.

Remember the worst murder that has ever been perpetrated upon this earth was the killing of the innocent Son of God. Some day that crime must be reckoned with. Judgment must come on those who have rejected the Son of God and put Him to an open shame. God will judge every person who has rejected His Son. We as Christians look for Christ, because our Saviour is coming to receive us to Himself and free us from this day of judgment.

FOUR HORSEMEN

In the sixth chapter we see the famous "four horsemen." (6:1-8) Restraint is removed as the seals are broken. The forces of evil have been held in check. When the seals are torn away, war and destruction are set loose. The terrible possibilities of a godless society ride forth unchallenged.

We cannot blame God for what man has brought upon himself. Men have been setting themselves up independently of God. They have been heaping up power. They have been building for war, and torture is let loose. They are destroying their makers. Why blame God for this? Man is reaping what he has sown himself. The anguish and horror of the period will be the result of human ambition, hatred, and cruelty. All that God does is to remove restraint.

First, we see the white horse of religious witness, come before the final catastrophe upon the earth. Then comes the red horse, and universal war breaks upon the world, *when peace will be taken from the earth*. This means world war. The black horse of famine and scarcity follows upon universal war. We know that war brings breadlines and soup kitchens. Lastly, the pale horse of pestilence and death comes forth with merciless tread.

The sixth seal (6:12-17) brings social chaos, the complete breaking up of society and a boasted civilization. Darkness, falling stars, heavens rolled up as a scroll, islands moving is the picture presented. Then the most tragic prayer meeting on earth with kings and priests, rich and poor, fleeing from God in a general stampede, praying for death, for *the great day of His wrath is come*. Man fancies himself able to overturn civil government and to establish a millennium of his own, but it results in the worst social chaos the world will ever see. Man has played with war until the very foundations of civilization rock to pieces. Frightened men of all classes flee for shelter from the oncoming cataclysm.

THE SEVEN TRUMPETS

Silence in heaven for thirty minutes! Orchestras cease! Seraphim and cherubim fold their wings! All is still! It is as though all heaven were waiting in breathless expectation. This is the calm before the storm. (chap. 8) War, famine and pestilence have devastated the earth. Millions of people have died. Now all hell is set loose on the earth. Men have chosen sin and Satan, instead of righteousness and a Redeemer. Now His judgments have come upon the earth and Satan, knowing his time is short, is exceedingly wrathful. We find unprecedented activity of demons, 200,000,000 evil spirits sweeping across the earth. Hell is let loose! Sin is allowed its full sway, and death is preferable to life. (9:1-21) Satan does his last work upon the earth.

FEDERATION OF NATIONS

Finally we see Satan incarnating himself in the Antichrist. His portrait is given in Revelation 13. See also Daniel 12:11; Matt. 24:15; II Thess. 2:3. This Antichrist will be a world ruler. He demands the honors due to Christ Himself. He will be the political ruler of this world. He is the embodiment of wickedness. He will be shrewd and clever and a real leader of men. The

Antichrist will be a Caesar, an Alexander, a Nero and a Hitler all in one. He will be the world's superman. Men can neither *buy nor sell, save he that hath the mark*. Mergers and trusts of great proportion are in the world today. Such mergers and trusts were unheard of at the beginning of this century. The *mark of the beast* is like the brand mark of ownership, or the token of allegiance like the swastika. It will be impossible for man to buy or sell without permission. The number 666 is "the number of a man." 6 is the number of evil. So three 6's express a trinity of wickedness.

The final doom of the Antichrist will be the lake of fire at Christ's coming. (19:20) There will be plagues like those of Egypt—blood, hail, fire, locusts, darkness, famine, sores, earthquakes, war and death. In these plagues is summed up the wrath of God upon a Christ-rejecting world.

THE SEVEN GOLDEN BOWLS

In the trumpets, Satan is releasing his power to accomplish his objectives. The bowls are God's power released against Satan. The bowls are God's answer to the Devil. The "bowls" blast the dominion of Satan. Satan has dared to challenge God's power. God is now answering the challenge. Satan is forced into action. His kingdom is shaken to its foundations and he is undone. This event ends in the Battle of Armageddon. (16:13-16) This battle is described in chapter 19. This is the closing scene of the war, when Christ takes the leadership of His armies, and brings His foes to their doom. In the "bowls" the power of the Almighty has been unleashed.

The seventh "bowl" announced the "Dooms" which were to follow. Civilization has come to utter collapse. Even though God has revealed its utter evil, neverthe-less men blaspheme God and repent not. (16:9,11) Even today, amid the luxuries of inventions, men are dissatisfied and far from God. Hatred has turned into wars of colossal dimension. God pronounces seven "Dooms." (chapters 17-20) First the doom of great systems—ecclesiastical (chap. 17), commercial (chap. 18), political (19:11-19); then the Beast and the False Prophet (19:20,21), followed by the nations (20:7-9), and the Devil (20:10), and finally, the doom of the lost is pronounced (20:11-15).

THE MARRIAGE OF THE LAMB

The "Hallelujah Chorus" announces the coming of the long-promised King, our Lord Jesus Christ, the heir of David's throne to catch away His bride. (I Thess. 4:17) Hell has been let loose on earth. Satan and his cohorts have done their worst, and Christ has finally triumphed. Righteousness, long on the scaffold, is now to mount the throne. The marriage of the Lamb is come. (19:7) The marriage supper of Christ will take place in the air. The saints will be rewarded in the air, according to their works. This time of rejoicing will continue until Christ returns to the earth with His bride, to set up His millennial kingdom.

DOOM OF THE ANTICHRIST

After the Battle of Armageddon (19:17-19), Christ having subdued all His enemies, will take alive Antichrist (19:20) and the False Prophet and cast them with a strong arm into the lake of fire. This is a name for Gehenna, the place where torment never ceases and from which none return. Christ will make an end of Satan's entire system.

THE MILLENNIUM

This is the time when Christ, the Prince of Peace, will establish His kingdom upon the earth for a thousand years (20:2,3); the saints that Christ brings with Him will reign with Him for a thousand years

(20:4,6); the wicked dead will not rise until the end of the thousand years (20:5).

There will be a thousand years of peace and joy upon the earth, when *the earth shall be filled with the knowledge of the glory of the Lord, as the waters cover the sea.* (Hab. 2:14). It will be a glorious time to live. No wars, no weeds, no wild animals, no taxes, neither the heartache of death! When this period has come to an end, then the Devil will be released again. He will come to test the nations. (20:7-9) We discover their real attitude, and learn that they prefer Satan to Christ. We can hardly believe it, but read 20:7-9: *And when the thousand years are expired, Satan shall be loosed out of his prison, and shall go out to deceive the nations which are in the four quarters of the earth, Gog and Magog, to gather them together to battle: the number of whom is as the sand of the sea.*

Satan is the author and instigator of war. After a thousand years of peace, Satan gathers them to "the war." Not a few gather, but a countless number, *like the sand of the sea.* But *fire came down from God out of heaven, and devoured them* (20:9). Men's rebellion against God seems almost unbelievable but *the heart is deceitful above all things, and desperately wicked: who can know it?* (Jer. 17:9)

SATAN GETS A LIFE SENTENCE

Satan is treated too lightly by the average person. He is mighty! He is *the deceiver of the whole world.* He fell from the highest place, next to God Himself, to the lowest depths—*the lake of fire.* Christ described it as *everlasting fire prepared for the devil and his angels* (Matt. 25:41). The Devil is given a life sentence. (Rev. 20:10)

A DEADLINE FOR THE SOUL

The blazing white throne of the final judgment is set.

The One sitting upon it shall judge all men. Read Revelation 20:11-15. He summons the Grand Jury to begin their hearings. The doom of the lost is reserved to the last. The innumerable host assembled for this last solemn assize makes us shudder. The "dead" are brought before Him. The sea gives up its dead. The grave gives up its dead. Hades gives up the dead. The dead are judged according to their works. (20:12,13) Final doom is pronounced. The erstwhile Saviour is now the Judge. *Whosoever was not found written in the book of life was cast into the lake of fire* (20:15). Judgment must come before the Golden Age of glory can be ushered in. Someone has called hell the penitentiary of the universe, and the universe cemetery of the spiritually dead.

SEVEN NEW THINGS

A new heaven and earth...........................21:1
A new people...................................21:2-8
A new bride....................................21:9
A new home..................................21:10-21
A new temple 21:22
A new light...................................21:23-27
A new Paradise 22:1-5

God's story ends "and they lived happily ever after." Read the triumph of God in Revelation 21 and 22. Satan has not been victorious in his attempt to separate man from fellowship with God by sin, ever since his meeting with the first man and woman in the garden of Eden. He has utterly failed and we will be with Christ forever and ever!

Don't try to analyze or interpret this great scene. Rather, meditate upon it. This is heaven! How limited words are in explaining its glory! The fellowship between God and man is restored. God *dwells with His people*. Every purpose is realized and every promise is fulfilled. Heaven is the opposite of what we experience

270

here. No tears in heaven—much weeping here. No death in heaven—separation here. No night in heaven! Darkness gathers here.

There is a longing, deep in the heart of humanity, for a better life and a better world than this. Innumerable trials have been made to settle the world's problems and woes, but all have failed. As long as man has occupied the throne, righteousness has been on the scaffold. But this failure is not the end! Heaven is a real place and some day those who are Christians will live there.

The last words of Christ in His Revelation are *Surely I come* (22:20). Our response should ever be, *Even so, come* (22:20).

Is this your sincere prayer? Are you sure of His blessing? Is He the Alpha and Omega of your life—the end of all for you? Make Him so now. If not, the days ahead will be dark and full of fear for you. You must do something with Christ. He is either your Saviour or your Judge. He will save or condemn.

"BOOK at a GLANCE"
Revelations

Past (1:1-18)

What "sevens" are presented in Revelation?......................

....

How is Christ pictured in all of Revelation?......................

....

In what chapter and verse do we find the outline of this book? ....

....

Present (1:20–3:22)

Name the seven churches mentioned in chapters 2 and 3. ....

....

Where is Christ found at the end of the church age?

....

Future (4:1–22:21)

What persons are presented in the court scene of chapter 4?...
....

What are "the four horsemen of the apocalypse"?..........
....

Where do we find the picture of the Antichrist as the world's political leader?...

Who is the leader in the battle of Armageddon?............

Where do we find the time given for the millennium?
....

What happens to the Devil and his angels?.....................
....

What is the last prayer in the Bible?...............................
....

Minimum Daily Requirements / Spiritual Vitamins

Sunday: CHRIST AND THE CHURCHES Revelation 1:1–3:22

Monday: CHRIST'S THRONE AND THE SEVEN SEALED BOOKS Revelation 4:1–6:17

Tuesday: CHRIST'S TRUMPETS SOUNDED Revelation 7:1–9:21

Wednesday: CHRIST AND THE WOES Revelation 10:1–12:17

Thursday: CHRIST AND ANTICHRIST Revelation 13:1–15:8

Friday: CHRIST'S FINAL TRIUMPH Revelation 16:1–18:24

Saturday: CHRIST THE LORD OF ALL Revelation 19:1–22:21

Chapter 26

A QUICK LOOK
AT THE NEW TESTAMENT
COLOSSIANS THROUGH REVELATION

OUTSTANDING TRUTHS
Two Minute Reports

Christ's second coming
Twentieth century false religions
Christ the head of the church
The power of a Christian life
The word "better" in Hebrews
Power of the tongue

WHAT EPISTLES ARE SUGGESTED BY THE FOLLOWING WORDS?

Righteousness
Christ's coming again
The unruly tongue
The good fight (the wrestler)
Christian love

BIOGRAPHIES
Two Minute Talks

James   Timothy
Peter   Philemon
John, the apostle   Titus

WHAT WAS THE OCCASION OF EACH OF THE FOLLOWING STATEMENTS?

In What Book Is It Found?

I have fought a good fight, I have finished my course, I have kept the faith: henceforth there is laid up for me a crown of righteousness, which the Lord, the righteous judge, shall give me.

The Lord Himself shall descend from heaven with a shout, with the voice of the archangel, . . . and the dead in Christ shall rise first . . .

Come boldly unto the throne of grace.

Blessed is he that readeth, and they that hear the words of this prophecy and keep those things which are written therein; for the time is at hand.

What have you learned about the Second Coming of Christ in the Epistles?

How is Christ portrayed in each Book?

What is the Message in Each?

TEST YOURSELF ON THE LETTERS IN THE NEW TESTAMENT

Place a check mark in the square you think is the correct answer.

	False	True
All the letters of the New Testament were written by Paul.	☐	☐
Timothy wrote the book called by his name.	☐	☐
Peter wrote only one epistle.	☐	☐

GREAT SENTENCE REVIEW

This gives a study of the most notable sentences in the epistles we have studied the past weeks. Pick out the ones that seem most important to you and comment upon them. (Use concordance if necessary.)

All scripture is given by inspiration of God.

Now faith is the substance of things hoped for, the evidence of things not seen.

Faith without works is dead.

Unto you therefore which believe He is precious.

Add to your faith virtue; and to virtue knowledge.

If we confess our sins, He is faithful and just to forgive us our sins, and to cleanse us from all unrighteousness.

LAST WORDS ARE IMPORTANT
What were the last words of

Christt?   Luke 24:46-53
Paul?   II Timothy 4:1-9
Peter?   II Peter 3:10-18
James?   James 5:10-20
Jude?   Jude 17-25
The Bible?   Revelation 22:8-21

CHECK IN THE SQUARE YOUR CORRECT ANSWER

Thessalonians tells □ the sin of the tongue; □ of Christ's second coming; □ of Christ, the High Priest.

The heroes of the faith are found in □ Timothy; □ Hebrews; □ Revelation.

Timothy was □ Paul's son; □ an early missionary; □ Paul's convert.

God's future plans are revealed in □ Hebrews; □ Titus; □ Revelation.